good cooking

Marvelous Meat & Poultry

Published by:
R&R Publications Marketing Pty. Ltd
ACN 083 612 579
PO Box 254, Carlton North, Victoria 3054 Australia
Phone (61 3) 9381 2199 Fax (61 3) 9381 2689
E-mail: info@randrpublications.com.au
Web: www.randrpublications.com.au

©Richard Carroll
Good Cooking: Marvelous Meat and Poultry

Publisher: Richard Carroll
Creative Director: Lucy Adams
Production Manager: Anthony Carroll
Computer Graphics: Lucy Adams
Food Photography: Steve Baxter, Phillip Wilkins, David Munns, Thomas Odulate, Christine Hanscomb, Gary Smith, Warren Webb and Frank Wieder
Home Economist: Sara Buenfeld, Emma Patmore, Nancy McDougall, Louise Pickford, Jane Stevenson, Oded Schwartz, Alison Austin and Jane Lawrie
Food Stylists: Helen Payne, Sue Russell, Sam Scott, Antonia Gaunt Ellen Argyriou and Oded Schwartz
Recipe Development: Terry Farris, Jacqueline Bellefontaine, Ellen Argyriou Becky Johnson, Valerie Barrett, Emma Patmore, Geri Richards, Pam Mallender, Jan Fullwood and Tamara Milstein-(www.tamaraskitchen.com) (pages 28, 42, 68, 72, 128 and 326)
Nutritional Consultant: Moya de Wet BSc SRD
Proof Reader: Fiona Brodribb

All rights reserved. No part of this book may be stored, reproduced or transmitted in any form or by any means without written permission of the publisher, except in the case of brief quotations embodied in critical articles and reviews.

Includes Index
ISBN 1 74022 259 8
EAN 9 781740 22259 4

First Edition Printed September 2003
Computer Typeset in Times New Roman, Verdana, Helvetica, Shelley Allegro and Humanist
Printed in Singapore by Saik Wah Press Pte Ltd

good cooking

Contents

MARVELOUS MEAT & POULTRY	**4**
Meat Storage & Cooking Guide	6
Chicken Storage & Cooking Guide	8
Beef	10
Beef Appetizers, Snack, & Salads	12
Beef Mains	30
Lamb	64
Lamb Appetizers, Snacks, & Salads	66
Lamb Mains	78
Pork	108
Pork Appetizers, Snacks, & Salads	110
Pork Mains	130
Sausages	160
Poultry	172
Poultry Appetizers, Snacks, & Salads	174
Poultry Mains	212
Turkey	296
Game	312
Index	334

Marvelous Meat, & Poultry

Meat Storage & Cooking Guide

Purchasing and Storage

The following tips will ensure that the meat you purchase stays at its best for the longest possible time. Fresh meat should be kept as dry as possible and should not sit in its own 'drip' during storage. Store meat in the coldest part of the refrigerator. This will be the bottom shelf if your refrigerator does not have a special meat compartment.

The more cutting and preparation meat has had, the shorter the storage time – for example, ground meat has a shorter storage time than chops or steaks.

When storing meat in the refrigerator, place a stainless steel or plastic rack in a dish deep enough to catch any drip from the meat. Unwrap the meat and place it on the rack in stacks of not more than three layers. Cover loosely with aluminum foil or waxed paper.

If your refrigerator has a special meat storage compartment, unwrap the meat, arrange in stacks of not more than three layers, and cover the meat loosely with aluminium foil or waxed paper.

If meat is to be used within two days of purchase, it can be left in its original wrapping. Store the package in the special meat compartment or the coldest part of the refrigerator. Meat that has been kept in the refrigerator for two to three days will be more tender than meat cooked on the day of purchase because the natural enzymes soften the muscle fibres.

Always store raw meat away from cooked meat or other cooked food. If your refrigerator does not have a special meat compartment, store the raw meat at the bottom of the refrigerator and the cooked meat at the top. Storing meat in this way prevents the raw meat from dripping onto the cooked meat and so lessens the likelihood of cross-contamination.

Raw and cooked meats both store well in the freezer, but as with any food to be frozen, it should be in good condition before freezing.

To prepare raw meat for freezing, cut into portions required for a single meal, such as a family meal. It is easier and more economical to take two packs out of the freezer for extra people than to cook too much through over-packing. If the meat is packed when you purchase it, remove it from the wrapping and repackage it in freezer bags or suitable freezing containers.

Storage guide

Ground meat and sausages	2 days
Cubed beef, lamb, and pork	3 days
Steaks, chops, and cutlets	4 days
Roasting joints (with bone in)	3–5 days
Roasting joints (boned and rolled)	2–3 days
Corned beef and pickled pork	7 days

Cooking Methods and Suitable Cuts

Cooking techniques can be divided into two groups: dry heat and moist heat methods. The moist heat methods are pot roasting, casseroling, braising, stewing, and simmering. The dry heat methods are pan-frying, stir-frying, crumb-frying, broiling, barbecuing, and oven roasting. The following guide will help you choose the correct cut of meat for the cooking technique you wish to use.

Pot Roast
Beef: blade, brisket, chuck, round, fresh silverside, skirt, topside
Lamb: forequarter (shoulder), shank
Veal: (shoulder) forequarter

Casserole
Beef: blade, brisket, chuck, round, spare ribs, shin, fresh silverside, skirt, topside
Lamb: best neck, forequarter (shoulder), neck chop, shank, shoulder chop
Veal: forequarter (shoulder) chop and steak, neck chop, knuckle
Pork: diced pork, leg steak

Braise
Beef: blade, brisket, chuck, round, spare ribs, shin, fresh silverside, skirt, topside
Lamb: best neck, forequarter (shoulder), neck chop, shank, shoulder chop
Veal: forequarter (shoulder) chop and steak, neck chop, knuckle
Pork: leg steak

Stew
Beef: blade, brisket, chuck, round, spare ribs, shin, fresh silverside, skirt, topside
Lamb: best neck, forequarter (shoulder) and neck chop, shank
Veal: forequarter (shoulder) chop and steak, neck chop, knuckle
Pork: diced pork

Simmer
Beef: corned (salted) silverside, corned (salted) brisket
Pork: pickled pork

Pan-Fry or Pan Cook
Beef: blade, fillet, round (minute), rump, rib eye, spare ribs, sirloin steak (T-bone)
Lamb: best neck chop and cutlet, chump, leg and mid loin chop, loin chop and cutlet
Veal: cutlet, leg steak, loin chop, schnitzel (escalope)
Pork: butterfly (valentine) steak, cutlet, fillet, forequarter (spare rib) chop and steak, leg steak, loin chop and medallion steak, schnitzel (escalope)

Stir-Fry
Beef: fillet, round, rump, rib eye, topside, sirloin (T-bone) steak
Lamb: boneless leg, boneless shoulder, boneless mid loin, fillet
Pork: diced pork, schnitzel (escalope)

Crumb-Fry
Beef: round (minute), topside steak
Lamb: best neck chop, rib loin cutlet
Veal: leg steak, schnitzel (escalope), loin chop, cutlet
Pork: schnitzel (escalope)

Broil
Beef: fillet, rump, rib eye, spare ribs, sirloin steak (T-bone steak)
Lamb: best neck chop and cutlet, chump, forequarter, leg and mid loin chop, rib loin chop and cutlet, shoulder chop
Veal: leg steak, loin chop and cutlet
Pork: butterfly (valentine) steak, cutlet, fillet, forequarter (spare rib) chop and steak, leg steak, loin chop and medallion steak, schnitzel (escalope), spare ribs

Barbecue
Beef: fillet, rump, rib eye, spare ribs, sirloin (T-bone) steak
Lamb: chump, forequarter, leg, shoulder and mid-loin chop, rib loin chop and cutlet
Veal: leg steak, loin chop and cutlet
Pork: boneless loin, butterfly (valentine) steak, cutlet, fillet, loin, forequarter (spare rib) chops and steak, leg steak, loin medallion steak, spare ribs

Oven Roast
Beef: fillet, rump, rib roast, spare ribs, sirloin, fresh silverside, topside
Lamb: breast, forequarter (shoulder), leg, mid loin, rib loin, rack, crown roast, shank
Veal: leg, loin, rack, forequarter (shoulder)
Pork: fillet, loin, leg, boneless loin, schnitzel (escalope), shoulder (hand or spring), spare ribs

Chicken Storage & Cooking Guide

Purchasing and Storage

Chicken may be purchased fresh or frozen; whole or in pieces. The choice is for the individual to make, depending on how and when one wishes to prepare and eat the chicken.

Fresh Chicken

- When purchasing fresh chicken, make it the last purchase on your shopping trip. It is advisable to take along an insulated bag to place the chicken in to keep it cold on the trip home.
- Upon arriving home with the chicken, remove it from the package, rinse it and wipe it dry with a paper towel. Cover the chicken loosely with plastic wrap and refrigerate immediately. Fresh chicken may be kept in the refrigerator for 3 days. Place in the coldest part of the refrigerator, below 39°F/4°C.
- If chicken needs to be stored longer, it is better to buy ready-frozen chicken than to buy fresh chicken and freeze it at home.
- If the chicken pieces are to be purchased and frozen for future use, make sure they are fresh. Wipe dry with paper towel then pack flat in plastic freezer bags. Extract the surrounding air by pushing out towards the opening, and tape the bag closed. Label and date the packages.

Frozen Chicken

- When purchasing frozen chicken, check that the packages are not torn.
- Place in the freezer immediately when you return home.
- Thaw frozen chicken thoroughly before cooking to avoid toughening the texture, and to reduce the chance of some parts being undercooked. Undercooked parts could harbor food-spoiling bacteria.
- Do not re-freeze thawed chicken. It is advisable to cook the thawed chicken and freeze it when cooked.
- To thaw frozen chicken, remove from wrap, and place on a rack in a dish to allow any liquid to collect beneath the chicken. Do not touch the chicken. Cover loosely with plastic wrap and place in the refrigerator for 24 hours. This is the safest way to thaw chicken. Thawing on the kitchen bench encourages the growth of bacteria and should be avoided.

Cooking Methods and Suitable Cuts

Roasting
Whole chicken, drumsticks, maryland thighs, breast on the bone, lovely legs

Broiling and Barbecuing
No. 8–10 chicken cut in half, thigh cutlets, breast on the bone, maryland

Pan Frying
Breast fillet, thigh fillets, stir-fry, tenderloin

Casseroling and Stewing
Chicken pieces, breast on the bone, thighs, thigh cutlets, maryland, drumsticks, lovely legs

Simmering
Whole chicken, breast on the bone, thighs

Tips

Because raw poultry may carry potentially harmful organisms, careful handling of any uncooked bird is of particular importance. Always wash hands, preparations surfaces, and utensils in hot, soapy water before and after preparing raw poultry

A serving of lean beef (approximately 4 oz/125 g) is a good nutritional parcel. It will give you about 30 percent of your daily requirement and protein which contains all of the eight essential amino acids. It will also give you approximately 20 per cent of the recommended daily allowance of iron.

Beef

Beef Appetizers, Snacks, & Salads

Mini Beef and Pine Nut Meat Loaves

Ingredients

cooking oil spray

15 oz/480 g lean ground beef

1 small onion, finely grated

1 small carrot, finely grated

2 tbsp pine nuts, toasted

1 tsp mixed dried herbs

1 egg, lightly beaten

1 cup fresh breadcrumbs

2 tbsp reduced-salt tomato ketchup

Method

1 Preheat the oven to 350°F/180°C/Gas Mark 4. Spray 4 large (8¾ fl oz/250 mL) muffin tins with cooking spray.

2 Put the ground beef, onion, carrot, pine nuts, herbs, egg and breadcrumbs in a bowl and mix to combine.

3 Divide the mixture among the four greased muffin tins and press in firmly. Spread the tops with the tomato sauce and bake for 30 minutes or until cooked through. Each meat loaf will start to come away from the edges of its tin when cooked.

4 Serve hot or cold with whole-wheat bread and salad.

Serves 4

Thai Beef Salad

Ingredients

1 lb 6 oz/750 g rump or sirloin steak
freshly ground pepper
1/2 cup mint leaves
1 large red onion or 2 large scallions, thinly sliced
2 red chilies, halved, seeded and very finely shredded
juice of 1 large lime or 1/2 lemon
2 tbsp fish sauce
1 tsp sugar
lettuce leaves, whole or halved, cherry tomatoes and extra mint leaves to garish

Method

1 Season the steak with pepper and cook under a preheated broiler for 5 minutes on until each side or done to taste. Remove, cut into very thin slices, and place in a bowl.

2 Meanwhile, combine the mint leaves with the onion slices, finely shredded chilies, lime or lemon juice, fish sauce and sugar. Stir well, and add to the beef slices, tossing to combine. Arrange on a salad platter garnish with the lettuce leaves, cherry tomatoes and extra mint leaves and serve.

Serves 4–6

Beef Carpaccio

Ingredients
freshly ground black pepper
salt
14 oz/450 g beef fillet, sliced into 1/4 in/4 mm slices
4 oz/125 g arugula, washed
3 tsp balsamic vinegar
1 1/2 fl oz/45 mL extra virgin olive oil
pecorino cheese shavings

Method
1 Lightly oil a sheet of waxed paper and season it lightly with salt, and freshly ground black pepper.

2 Arrange 4 slices of beef on the paper (approximately 2 in/5 cm apart). Place another oiled piece of waxed paper on top, and gently beat the meat, until it has spread out to at least twice its former size. Repeat with the remaining meat slices.

3 Refrigerate until needed. Alternatively, partly freeze the meat slice thinly it.

4 Place some arugula in the center of a plate, arrange the beef slices around the arugula, and drizzle with some balsamic vinegar and olive oil.

5 Serve topped with shavings of pecorino cheese and black pepper.

Serves 6

Individual Beef and Red Wine Pies

Ingredients

2 tsp peanut oil

1 large onion, chopped

2 cloves garlic, crushed

2 lb 2 oz/1 kg beef chuck steak trimmed of all fat and cubed

2 tbsp all-purpose flour

2 tbsp reduced-salt tomato paste

1 1/2 cups red wine

1 1/2 cups reduced salt beef bouillon

2 carrots, thinly sliced

7 oz/200 g Swiss brown mushrooms, quartered

2 tbsp fresh thyme, chopped

2 tbsp fresh parsley, chopped

2 sheets canola puff pastry, defrosted

4 sprigs thyme

1 tbsp low- or reduced-fat milk

Method

1 Preheat the oven to 400°F/200°C/Gas Mark 5. You will need 6 x 2 cup capacity ovenproof pie dishes.

2 Heat the oil in a large saucepan, add the onion, and cook over a medium heat for 5 minutes or until golden. Add the garlic and the beef and cook for 5 minutes until the beef is browned.

3 Add the flour and tomato paste and cook for a further 2 minutes, stirring constantly. Stir in the red wine and bouillon and bring to the boil. Add the carrots, mushrooms and chopped thyme. Reduce the heat, cover and simmer for about 1 hour then remove the lid and cook for a further 45 minutes until the beef is tender and the sauce is reduced and thickened. Stir through the parsley, transfer to a bowl and allow the filling to cool completely.

4 Using the top of a pie dish as a guide, cut 6 circles from the pastry, about 3/4 in/2 cm larger than the dish. Spoon the cooled filling into the dishes. Brush the edges of each pastry circle with a little water then cover the dishes (damp side down), pressing the pastry to the side of the dish to seal. Cut a small cross in the top of each pie, insert a sprig of thyme and lightly brush with milk.

5 Bake for 20–25 minutes or until the pastry is crisp and golden and the filling is hot. Serve the pies with mashed potato and steamed beans.

Serves 6

Beef-Filled Cucumber Boats with Dipping Sauce

Ingredients

Beef Filling

1 red onion

2 cloves garlic

salt, to taste

½ cup brown rice

½ cup wild rice

1 tbsp peanut oil

2 tbsp minced ginger

1 small red chili

1 lb/500 g lean ground beef

1 tsp cumin

1 tbsp mild curry powder

2 tsp fish sauce

2 cups Italian tomato-based pasta sauce

½ bunch fresh cilantro

4–6 large cucumbers

Sauce

2 tbsp sour cream or yogurt

juice of 1 lemon

juice of 2 limes

1 bunch fresh cilantro, chopped

2 tbsp sweet chili sauce

3 tbsp fish sauce

2 tbsp peanut oil

Method

1 Preheat the oven to 340°F/170°C/Gas Mark 4. Roughly chop the onion and ground beef the garlic. Bring a medium-sized saucepan of water to the boil, add salt to taste, then cook the wild rice and brown rice together for 20 minutes (until firm but tender). Drain the rice and run under cold water (to halt the cooking time). Set aside.

2 Heat the peanut oil and sauté the onion, garlic, minced ginger, and chili, until the onion has softened and the mixture is aromatic. Add the minced beef and cook over a high heat, stirring constantly to break up the meat. Continue cooking until the meat is cooked through and the liquid has evaporated. Add the cumin, curry powder, and fish sauce, and stir well.

3 Add the tomato sauce and simmer for 10 minutes or until the mixture is thick and fairly dry. Remove from the heat and fold the fresh chopped cilantro and cooked brown rice mixture through the cooked mixture. Meanwhile, make the sauce, process all the ingredients together and chill until ready to serve.

4 Wash the cucumbers, then cut them lengthways and scoop out all the seeds. Fill the cucumbers with the beef mixture, piling the beef. Place into a mound in a baking dish, nestling each one next to the previous one. Bake at 340°F/170°C/Gas Mark 4 for 15 minutes, then serve warm drizzled with the cilantro sauce. To make the sauce, process all the ingredients together and chill until ready to serve.

Serves 6–8

Lemon Grass Beef Parcels

Ingredients

2 oz/55 g Chinese (mung bean) vermicelli
12 oz/340 g lean ground beef
1/2 cup bean sprouts
2 stalks lemon grass, finely chopped
1 tbsp lemon juice
1 tbsp fish sauce
2 scallions, thinly sliced
7 oz/200 g can water chestnuts, drained and finely chopped
12 rice paper wrappers
12 fresh mint leaves
sweet chili sauce for dipping

Method

1 Put the vermicelli in a bowl, cover with boiling water and allow to stand for 10 minutes or until soft. Drain well.

2 Put the ground beef and 3 tablespoons of water in a frying pan and cook over a high heat for about 10 minutes or until the beef is tender and cooked. Drain off any excess liquid.

3 Transfer the beef to a bowl, add the bean sprouts, lemon grass, lemon juice, fish sauce, scallions and water chestnuts.

4 Soak the rice paper wrappers, one at a time, in a bowl of warm water until soft (or allow each guest a bowl of water and let them soak their own).

5 Place a mint leaf at the end of a wrapper, place 2 tablespoons of the beef mixture on the wrapper, fold in the ends, and roll up to enclose.

6 Serve with sweet chili sauce.

Makes 12

Steak and Kidney Puffs

Ingredients

4 tbsp groundnut oil
1 onion, finely chopped
1 lb/500 g braising steak, trimmed of excess fat and cubed
12 oz/350 g pig's kidney, halved, cores removed, then cut into $1/2$ in/1 cm pieces
3 tbsp all-purpose flour
1 tbsp tomato paste
2 tsp Worcestershire sauce
14 fl oz/400 mL beef bouillon
finely grated zest of 1 lemon
2 tbsp finely chopped fresh parsley, plus extra to garnish
1 tsp dried mixed herbs
salt and black pepper
5 oz/150 g baby button mushrooms
13 oz/375 g pack ready-rolled puff pastry
fresh rosemary to garnish

Method

1 Preheat the oven to 325°F/160°C/Gas Mark 3. Heat half the oil in a large flameproof casserole dish, add the onion, and cook for 5 minutes. Add half the steak and kidney and fry over a high heat, stirring, for 6 minutes, or until browned. Keep warm. Fry the remaining meat, adding more oil if necessary.

2 Return all the meat to the dish, add the flour, and stir for 2 minutes. Add the tomato paste, Worcestershire sauce, bouillon, lemon zest, herbs, and salt and pepper. Bring to the boil, stirring, then cover.

3 Transfer to the oven. After $1^{1}/_{2}$ hours, stir in the mushrooms and a little water, if needed. Cook for 35 minutes more. Meanwhile, unroll the pastry, and cut into 4 x $4^{1}/_{2}$ in/12 cm circles. Put on a baking sheet.

4 Take the casserole out of the oven. Increase the oven temperature to 400°F/200°C/Gas Mark 6. Meanwhile, place the casserole over a very low heat. Keep covered but stir occasionally. Bake the pastry for 20 minutes or until golden brown. Top each pastry circle with the steak and kidney. Garnish with herbs.

Serves 4

Chili Con Carne

Ingredients

1 onion, finely chopped

1 clove garlic, crushed

1 tbsp olive oil

1 lb/500 g extra-lean ground beef

1 jar (17½ oz/500 g) salsa dip

1 can (15 oz/425 g) three bean mix, drained

1 bay leaf

1 green bell pepper, finely chopped

½ cup concentrated beef bouillon

salt and pepper to taste

Method

1 Gently fry the onion and garlic in the olive oil until softened.

2 Add the ground beef and cook until it changes color.

3 Add the remaining ingredients and simmer for 40 minutes. Serve with pasta, rice or vegetables.

Note: Create nachos by lining a baking dish with corn chips, top with chili con carne and grated cheese. Bake in a medium oven for 20 minutes. Serve with grated cheese, sour cream and guacamole.

Serves 4

Mulligatawny

Ingredients

3½ oz/100 g dried chickpeas
3½ oz/100 g dried yellow split peas
3 tbsp ghee or butter
3 tbsp mild curry powder
3 tbsp garam masala
3 tbsp fresh minced ginger
3 cloves garlic, minced
4 large brown onions, diced
2 leeks, well washed and chopped
14 oz/400 g ground beef
3 medium carrots, grated
2 stalks celery, finely sliced
1 small cauliflower, divided into florets
1 bunch cilantro, chopped
8 cups chicken or beef bouillon
4 tbsp yogurt
salt and pepper, to taste

Method

1 Place the chickpeas and split peas in a large bowl of water and soak for 30 minutes. Drain. Heat the ghee or butter in a large saucepan and add the curry powder, garam masala, ginger, and garlic, and sauté until the spices are fragrant (about 3 minutes). Add the onions and leeks and cook over a medium-high heat until the onions have softened and are beginning to turn golden (about 6 minutes).

2 Add the ground beef and cook in the spice and onion mixture, making sure that the meat is thoroughly cooked and fragrant before continuing.

3 Add the carrots, celery, cauliflower, half the chopped cilantro, the bouillon and the chickpea mixture and bring to the boil. Simmer the soup for 1½ hours or until the chickpeas are tender, stirring often.

4 When almost ready to serve, stir through the yogurt and add salt and pepper to taste. Garnish with the remaining chopped cilantro and serve.

Serves 8-10

Beef Mains

Veal Saltimbocca

Ingredients

4 veal escalopes, each 4 oz/125 g
2–3 tbsp butter
7 oz/200 g mozzarella, sliced into 8 rounds
8 slices prosciutto
1 bunch of sage
2 tsp sage, roughly chopped
½ cup white wine
¼ cup chicken bouillon

Method

1 Using a meat mallet, pound the veal until thin.

2 Heat the butter in a pan, add the veal, and brown quickly on both sides. Remove veal from the pan, and set pan with juices asside. Top each piece of veal with 2 slices of mozzarella, 2 slices of prosciutto, and 2–3 sage leaves. Secure together with toothpicks.

3 Under a hot broiler, broil the veal for approximately 2 minutes, until the cheese has just started to melt. Reheat the pan and juices, add the sage, and cook for 1 minute. Add the white wine and chicken bouillon to pan and reduce the sauce slightly.

4 Pour the sauce over the veal, and serve immediately.

Serves 4

Veal with Lemon, Crisp Sage, and Cornmeal

Ingredients

2 cups reduced-salt chicken bouillon

1 cup instant cornmeal

4 large veal escalopes
   (thin, boneless slices)

all-purpose flour for dusting

2 tsp olive oil

²/₃ fl oz/20 g olive oil spread

3 fl oz/85 mL dry white wine

zest of 1 lemon

3 tbsp lemon juice

1 cup frozen broad beans,
   thawed and peeled

1 tbsp baby capers

1 tbsp chopped fresh parsley

12 fresh sage leaves

olive oil cooking spray

1 tbsp balsamic vinegar

3 Roma tomatoes, cut
   into thick slices

cracked black pepper, to taste

Method

1   Bring the chicken bouillon to the boil in a medium pot. Gradually whisk in the cornmeal and cook over a medium heat for 8 minutes or until the cornmeal starts to come away from the side of the pot. Cover and keep warm.

2   Dust the veal escalopes in flour, shaking off any excess. Heat the olive oil and olive oil spread in a large, deep frying pan, add the veal and cook over a medium heat until golden brown on both sides. (This will only take a couple of minutes on each side.) Remove and keep warm.

3   Add the wine to the pan and bring to the boil, stirring to remove any juices that may be stuck to the bottom. Boil until reduced by half. Add the lemon zest, juice, and broad beans and boil until the sauce has reduced and thickened slightly. Return the veal to the pan and heat through. Stir in the capers and chopped parsley.

4   Lightly spray the sage leaves with olive oil spray, grill until crisp and scatter over the veal.

5   Drizzle vinegar over the tomatoes and season with pepper. Serve the veal on the cornmeal and arrange the tomatoes on the side.

Serves 4

Sizzling Beef

Ingredients

- 1 lb/455 g rump steak, trimmed of any excess fat and cut into thin strips
- 2 tbsp soy sauce
- 2 tbsp rice wine or sherry
- 1½ tbsp cornstarch
- 1 tsp sugar
- 3 tbsp groundnut oil
- 5 oz/145 g broccoli, cut into bite-sized pieces
- 1 large red bell pepper, deseeded and cut into thin strips
- 2 cloves garlic, crushed
- 3 tbsp oyster sauce
- 7 fl oz/200 g fresh bean sprouts
- salt and black pepper

Method

1 Put the steak, soy sauce, rice wine or sherry, cornstarch, and sugar into a non-metallic bowl and mix thoroughly.

2 Heat 1 tablespoon of the oil in a wok or large heavy-based frying pan, add one-third of the beef mixture and stir-fry over a high heat for 2–3 minutes, until browned. Remove and cook the remaining beef in 2 more batches, adding a little more oil if necessary.

3 Heat the remaining oil in the pan, then add the broccoli and 6 tablespoons of water. Stir-fry for 5 minutes, then add the pepper and garlic, and stir-fry for a further 2–3 minutes, until the broccoli is tender but still firm to the bite.

4 Stir in the oyster sauce, return the beef to the wok and add the bean sprouts. Toss over a high heat for 2 minutes or until the beef is piping hot and the bean sprouts have softened slightly, then season.

Note: Before you start cooking this colorful stir-fry, make sure all your ingredients are cut into pieces of roughly the same shape and size so that they cook evenly.

Serves 4

Pastitsio

Ingredients
2 fl oz/60 mL oil
1 onion, sliced
2 lb/1 kg ground beef
2 tbsp tomato paste
14 oz/400 g can tomatoes
1 cup water
2 tsp oregano, chopped
1 tsp sugar
1 tbsp Worcestershire sauce
1 cinnamon stick
salt and pepper
14 oz/400 g penne, cooked
2 whole eggs
¾ cup grated Romano cheese

Béchamel Sauce
4 oz/125 g unsalted butter
3 tbsp flour
4 cups milk
8 oz/250 g Romano cheese
4 egg yolks

Method

1 Heat the oil and sauté the onion for 5 minutes. Add the ground beef meat and cook for 10 minutes, breaking up the ground beef with a fork as it cooks.

2 Add the tomato paste, tomatoes, water, oregano, sugar, Worcestershire sauce, and the cinnamon stick and bring to the boil. Simmer for 45 minutes or until mixture is cooked and sauce is thick. Add more water during cooking if needed. Season with salt and pepper.

3 To make the béchamel: melt the butter in a saucepan, add the flour, and cook for 3 minutes. Add the milk, and, stirring continuously, bring to the boil, then simmer until the sauce thickens to a good coating consistency. Add the cheese and four egg yolks to the sauce, mixing well, then season with salt and pepper.

4 In a large oven-proof dish, mix the penne and the ground beef meat together, and add two the eggs to the mixture. Pour the béchamel sauce over the top, sprinkle with the additional cheese, and bake in the oven for 30–45 minutes (until the top is golden brown and the pastitsio is set).

5 Cut into slices and serve, hot or cold, with a Greek salad.

Serves 10

37

Beef with Green Peppercorn Sauce and Potatoes

Ingredients

- **12 small kipfler or baby potatoes, scrubbed**
- **4 New York cut steaks or sirloin steaks**
- **2 tsp safflower oil**
- **1 cup white wine**
- **4 oz/125 g can green peppercorns, drained and lightly bruised**
- **1/3 cup reduced-fat sour cream**
- **12 chives, coarsely chopped**

Method

1 Steam or microwave the potatoes until tender, cut into thick slices and keep warm.

2 While the potatoes are cooking, trim the steaks of any excess fat or sinew. Heat the oil in a large fry pan, add the steaks and cook over a medium high heat until cooked to your liking, turning once. Remove and keep warm.

3 Add the white wine and peppercorns to the pan and boil over a high heat until reduced by half, scraping the bottom of the pan to remove any juices that may be stuck.

4 Stir in the sour cream and simmer until the sauce is thick enough to coat the back of a spoon.

5 Serve the steaks on top of the potatoes drizzled with peppercorn sauce and sprinkled with the chives.

Serves 4

Steak au Poivre

Ingredients

3 tbsp mixed peppercorns
**4 thick fillet steaks,
about 6 oz/170 g each**
2 tbsp olive oil
14 fl oz/400 mL red wine
4 fl oz/100 mL water
salt

Method

1 Crush the peppercorns with a pestle and mortar or the end of a rolling pin. Brush the steaks with 1 tablespoon of the oil, then press the peppercorns around the edge of each steak with your fingers.

2 Heat the remaining oil in a large heavy-based fry pan over a medium to high heat. Add the steaks and cook for 5–6 minutes, turning once, until cooked. (The cooking time will vary depending on the thickness of the steaks, so check that they are cooked to your liking before removing from the pan.)

3 Transfer the steaks to serving plates and keep warm. Lower the heat and slowly pour the wine into the pan, then add the of water. Bring to the boil, then cook for 4 minutes or until reduced by half, stirring constantly. Add salt to taste and spoon the sauce over the steaks to serve.

Note: Colourful mixed peppercorns give a modern twist to this classic French recipe. Serve with the red wine sauce, French fries or new potatoes, and a leafy salad.

Serves 4

Fire and Spice Risotto

Ingredients

5 tbsp olive oil

8 cloves garlic, minced

3 tsp fresh grated ginger

1 bunch of scallions, chopped

½ cup parsley, chopped

½ cup cilantro, chopped

2 small red chilies, minced

2 tsp cumin

2 tsp ground cilantro

2 tsp tumeric

1 lb 12 oz/800 g skirt steak or cubed goulash beef

14 oz/400 g arborio rice

3½ fl oz/100 mL red wine

3½ fl oz/100 mL sherry

3 cups beef bouillon, simmering

2 tomatoes, chopped

2 tbsp lime juice

¼ cup parsley, chopped

⅓ cup yogurt

1 finely sliced onion, deep-fried

extra parsley

Method

1 Heat 4 tablespoons of the olive oil and add the garlic, ginger, scallops, herbs and spices. Sauté gently until the vegetables have softened and the mixture is aromatic. Add the beef and continue to sauté until the beef changes colour, about 5 minutes. Set aside.

2 In a separate saucepan, heat the remaining tablespoon of olive oil and add the arborio rice. Stir to coat, then add the red wine and sherry, simmering until the liquid has been absorbed. Begin to add the beef bouillon, half a cup at a time, stirring well after each addition and allowing each to be absorbed before adding the next quantity. When one quarter of the bouillon has been added, add the chopped tomatoes and the beef mixture, including all the liquid and spices, and continue to cook until the liquid has been absorbed. Continue adding bouillon in the usual manner until all the bouillon has been added and absorbed.

3 Remove the pan from the heat and add the lime juice and parsley, stirring well. Serve in individual bowls, garnished with a little yogurt, a mound of fried onions and a sprinkling of parsley.

Serves 4

Meat-Lovers' Pizza

Ingredients
8 oz/250 g very lean ground beef
sprinkle of seasoned pepper
salt
2 tbsp tomato salsa dip
shredded, light cheese
sprinkle of chives, chopped
fresh parsley, chopped
sprinkle of ground paprika

Method
1 Heat an electric fry pan on high until hot. Line with baking paper. Press the ground beef onto the baking paper to form the base of the pizza. Sprinkle with seasoned pepper and salt to taste. Cook, covered, on high until the ground beef changes color. Turn the meat and continue to cook for a few minutes.

2 Place the salsa, cheese, chopped chives, parsley and paprika onto the ground beef and cook, covered, on medium covered, for 5–7 minutes or until the cheese melts.

Serve with vegetables as a main meal or with salad as a snack with crusty bread.

Serves 4

Beef with Wine Sauce

Ingredients
1 1/2 lb/750 g eye fillet beef, in one piece
1 oz/30 g butter
1 onion, chopped
1 clove garlic, crushed
1 carrot, chopped
1 stalk celery, chopped
1 cup beef bouillon
1/4 cup red wine
3 tbsp tomato paste
freshly ground black pepper

Method
1 Tie the fillet with string to hold in shape. Melt the butter in a large fry pan and cook the fillet over a high heat until browned on all sides. Transfer to a baking dish and cook for 30 minutes or until cooked to your liking.

2 Add the onion, garlic, carrot and celery to the fry pan and cook, stirring constantly, for 5 minutes. Stir in the bouillon, wine and tomato paste bouillon, bring to the boil, then reduce, heat and simmer for 5 minutes or until the sauce reduces and thickens slightly. Season to taste with black pepper.

3 To serve, slice the meat and arrange on a serving platter, then spoon the sauce over.

Serves 4

Meat Lovers Pizza

Ground Beef Pie

Ingredients

1 lb/500 g very lean ground beef
1 medium onion, finely chopped
salt and pepper, to taste
1 tsp mixed herbs
1 cup water
Parisienne essence to color
2 tbsp all-purpose flour, mixed to a paste with water

Method

1 Place the ground beef, half the onion, and the salt and pepper, mixed herbs, water and a few drops of Parisienne essence into a saucepan and bring to the boil.

2 Reduce the heat to a simmer, cover the saucepan and cook for 30 minutes.

3 Add the rest of the onion. Add the flour mixture to the ground beef, a little at a time, until thickened. Adjust the seasonings if necessary.

Serves 4

Glazed Corned Beef

Ingredients

3 lb/1 1/2 kg corned (salted) silverside
2 tbsp brown sugar
1 tbsp cider vinegar
2 sprigs fresh mint
1 onion, peeled and studded with 4 whole cloves
6 black peppercorns
6 small carrots
6 small onions
3 parsnips, halved

Redcurrant Glaze

1/2 cup redcurrant jelly
2 tbsp orange juice
1 tbsp sweet sherry

Method

1 Place the silverside in a large heavy-based saucepan. Add the sugar, vinegar, mint, clove-studded onion, peppercorns and enough water to cover meat. Cover, bring to the boil over a medium heat, then reduce the heat and simmer for 1 1/4–1 1/2 hours.

2 Add the carrots, onions and parsnips to the pan and simmer for 40 minutes longer or until the vegetables are tender.

3 To make the glaze, place the redcurrant jelly, orange juice and sherry in a small saucepan and cook over a low heat, stirring occasionally, until the jelly melts and the glaze is blended. Transfer the meat to a warm serving platter and brush with the glaze. Slice the meat and serve with vegetables and any remaining glaze.

Serves 4

Ground Beef Pie

Slowly Simmered Indonesian Beef Curry

Ingredients

- 2 stalks lemon grass
- 4 tbsp dried coconut
- 2 onions, chopped
- 2 cloves garlic, chopped
- 2 in/5 cm piece fresh root ginger, chopped
- 1 red chili, deseeded and chopped, plus 1 red chili, deseeded and sliced, to garnish
- 2 tbsp vegetable oil
- 1 1/2 lb/675 g topside beef, cut into 2 1/2 cm/1 in cubes
- 1 tsp turmeric
- 14 fl oz/400 mL can coconut milk
- 1 tsp sugar
- salt

Method

1 Peel the outer layers from the lemon grass stalks, then finely chop the lower white bulbous parts discarding the fibrous tops. Heat a large saucepan and dry-fry the coconut for 5 minutes or until golden, stirring frequently. Finely grind the coconut in a food processor or use a pestle and mortar.

2 Blend or grind the lemon grass, onions, garlic, ginger and chili to a paste. Heat the oil in the pan and fry the paste for 5 minutes to release the flavors, stirring often. Add the beef, stir to coat and fry for 3–4 minutes or until sealed.

3 Add the ground coconut, turmeric, coconut milk, sugar and salt to taste, and mix well. Bring to the boil, stirring, then reduce the heat. Simmer uncovered for 3 hours, stirring from time to time, until the sauce reduces to a rich gravy. Garnish with the sliced chili. Serve with rice.

Note: This classic Indonesian dish, can also be made with lamb or venison. Slow cooking in the rich coconut sauce results in meltingly tender meat.

Serves 4

Peppered Beef Steaks with Red Onion Salsa

Ingredients

2 tbsp mixed peppercorns
1 tbsp olive oil
4 lean sirloin, rump, or fillet steaks, about 4 oz/115 g each, trimmed of fat
fresh parsley to garnish

Salsa

3 tomatoes
2 tbsp tomato juice
1 tbsp olive oil
1 red onion, finely chopped
2 tsp horseradish sauce
1 tbsp chopped fresh parsley
black pepper

Method

1 To make the salsa, place the tomatoes in a bowl, cover with boiling water and leave for 30 seconds. Drain, peel off the skins, deseed and finely chop. Place the flesh into a bowl with the tomato juice, the oil, red onion, horseradish, parsley and black pepper and mix together well. Cover and set aside for 1 hour.

2 Preheat the grill to medium. Crush the peppercorns with a pestle and mortar, or rolling pin. Brush the steaks all over of the oil, then coat with the crushed peppercorns.

3 Place the steaks on the grill rack and grill for 4–5 minutes on each side, until browned and cooked to your liking. Serve with the red onion salsa and garnish with fresh parsley.

Note: For a complete meal add warm tortillas, refried beans and a lettuce salad.

Serves 4

Boiled Beef and Vegetables

Ingredients

¾ lb/350 g dried chickpeas

12 cups water

1 lb/500 g beef chuck steak

1 lb/500 g large chicken thighs

¼ lb/115 g salt pork or slab bacon

¼ lb/115 g cured ham, such as prosciutto, in a thick slice

1 beef bone

salt and freshly ground pepper

¼ lb/115 g chorizo sausage or other mild or breakfast sausage

1 large carrot

2 large whole garlic cloves plus 1 minced, clove

1 turnip, halved

1 large leek, well washed

1 small whole onion plus 3 tbsp chopped onion

2 parsley sprigs

a few threads of saffron

6 small red potatoes, skin on

2 tbsp olive oil

1 small green cabbage, coarsely chopped

3 oz/85 g very thin noodles, such as fideos

Method

1 Cover the chickpeas with cold water and soak overnight.

2 In a large soup pot, combine the water, beef, chicken, salt pork, ham, beef bone, and salt and pepper. Bring to boil, cover and simmer the 1½ hrs. Let cool and refrigerate overnight if you wish to remove the fat that solidifies.

3 Drain and the rinse chickpeas. Add to the soup pot (preferably in a string bag to keep them together) with the chorizo, carrot, whole garlic, turnip, leek, whole onion, parsley, and saffron. Bring to the boil, cover and simmer about 2 hours, or until the chickpeas are almost tender. Add the potatoes and cook for 30 minutes more. Taste for salt.

4 Meanwhile, prepare the cabbage. Heat the oil in a large skillet and sauté minced garlic and chopped onion over a medium-high heat until the onion is wilted. Add the cabbage, season with salt and pepper, and stir-fry for 5 minutes. Cover, lower the heat, and cook for 5 minutes more. Cook the noodles in a separate pan of boiling salted water until just done; drain.

5 To serve, strain the broth, returning enough of it to the pot to keep the remaining ingredients moist. Combine the broth with the noodles and serve as a first course.

6 Cut the meat and vegetables into serving pieces. Arrange with the cabbage on 1 or 2 large platters with the chickpeas heaped in the center.

Serves 6

Pasta Bake

Ingredients

- 1 large onion, chopped
- 1 clove garlic, crushed
- 5 oz/145 g lean bacon, chopped
- 3 large mushrooms, chopped
- 1 tsp ground paprika
- 1 tsp oregano leaves
- 1 tbsp olive oil
- 1 lb/500 g lean ground beef
- 1 jar (10 oz/285 g) salsa dip – favorite variety
- 1/2 red bell pepper, chopped
- 1 cup freshly chopped basil leaves
- 2 bay leaves
- 1 lb/500 g spaghetti, cooked and drained
- 1 lb/500 g grated tasty cheese

Topping

- 1 cup grated cheese
- 2 eggs, beaten
- 1 cup fresh breadcrumbs, toasted

Method

1 Fry the onion, garlic, bacon, mushrooms, paprika and oregano in the olive oil until softened.

2 Add the ground beef and cook over a high heat until it changes color and breaks into small pieces.

3 Add the salsa, bell pepper, basil and bay leaves. Simmer for 30 minutes.

4 Preheat the oven to 350°F/180°C/Gas Mark 4. Layer the spaghetti with the meat sauce and cheese into a large, shallow baking dish.

5 To make the topping, combine the cheese with the eggs. Pour over the top of spaghetti bake, then sprinkle with the breadcrumbs.

6 Bake for 30 minutes or until golden brown. Cut into large squares and serve with a crisp green salad.

Serves 4

Creamy Pepper Steak

Ingredients
1 tbsp butter
1 lb/500 g rump steak, trimmed
sprinkle of seasoned pepper
1 tbsp fresh chopped
  parsley and chives
3 tbsp cream
salt and pepper, to taste

Method
1 Pre-heat an electric fry pan. Line it with baking paper. When hot, put the butter into the pan, on top of the baking paper.

2 Add the rump steak and lightly sprinkle with seasoned pepper. Cook until lightly browned, then turn and lightly sprinkle this side with the seasoned pepper.

3 Before the rump steak is cooked, add the parsley and chives and then add the cream. If you want a lot of sauce, add all the cream. If only a little sauce is required, add only 1 or 2 tablespoons of cream.

4 Turn the rump steak several times in the sauce, season to taste, then serve.

Serves 4

Moroccan Stew

Ingredients
1 tbsp vegetable oil
1 lb/500 g chuck steak, cut into
  1 in/2½ cm cubes
2 cups beef bouillon
2 tsp ground cinnamon
2 tbsp honey
½ tsp ground turmeric
½ tsp ground nutmeg
2 oz/60 g raisins
2 oz/60 g dried apricots, chopped
8 baby onions
2 tbsp orange juice
2 oz/60 g blanched almonds
freshly ground black pepper

Method
1 Heat the oil in a heavy-based saucepan and cook the meat over a high heat for 4–5 minutes or until browned on all sides. Stir in the bouillon and cinnamon, bring to the boil, then reduce the heat and simmer for 10 minutes, stirring to lift any sediment from the base of the pan.

2 Add the honey, turmeric, nutmeg, raisins and apricots to the pan, cover and simmer for 30 minutes.

3 Stir in the onions, orange juice and almonds and simmer, uncovered, for 30 minutes longer or until the meat is tender. Season to taste with black pepper.

Serves 4

Creamy Pepper Steak

Hearty Stew

Ingredients

2¼ lb/1 kg stewing steak, cubed
2 tbsp all-purpose flour
1 tsp sugar
3 onions, sliced
1 tsp freshly crushed garlic
7 oz/200 g lean bacon, finely chopped
1 tbsp olive oil
1 tbsp Worcestershire sauce
2 tbsp malt vinegar
1 jar (10 oz/300 g) salsa dip
freshly ground sea salt
freshly ground black pepper

Method

1 Coat the stewing steak in the flour and sugar and set aside.

2 Fry the onions, garlic and bacon in the olive oil until softened.

3 Add the stewing steak and cook for a few minutes to seal in the flavor.

4 Add the rest of the ingredients, season to taste, and simmer for 2 hours.

Serves 4

Mexican Meat Loaf

Ingredients

1 lb/500 g ground beef
2 tbsp or 1 oz/30 g packet taco seasoning mix
1 egg
1 cup breadcrumbs made from stale bread
4 oz/125 g tasty cheese (mature Cheddar), grated
1 cup taco sauce
1 oz/30 g corn chips

Method

1 Preheat the oven to 350°F/180°C/Gas Mark 4. Place the ground ground beef, taco seasoning mix, egg and breadcrumbs in a bowl and mix to combine. Press half the ground beef mixture into a lightly greased 11 cm x 21 cm/4½ in x 8½ in loaf tin. Top with half the grated cheese, then cover with remaining meat mixture. Bake for 40 minutes, then drain off any liquid, cover and set aside to stand for 10 minutes.

2 Turn the meat loaf onto an ovenproof plate, brush with taco sauce and top with the corn chips and remaining cheese. Bake at 400°F/200°C/Gas Mark 6 for 10 minutes or until the cheese is melted. Serve hot, warm or cold.

Serves 4

Hearty Stew

Spaghetti Bolognese

Ingredients

1 tbsp salt

14 oz/400 g dried spaghetti

2 oz/55 g fresh Parmesan cheese, grated, to serve

Sauce

1 tbsp vegetable oil or olive oil

1 medium onion, peeled and finely chopped

1 carrot, peeled and finely diced

1 stick celery, finely diced

2 cloves garlic, peeled and finely chopped

9 oz/250 g ground beef

2 x 14 oz/400 g cans chopped tomatoes

1 bay leaf

2 tsp dried oregano

1 tsp sugar

salt and black pepper

¼ cup red wine (optional)

Method

1 To make the sauce, put the oil in a medium-sized heavy-based saucepan and heat over a medium heat. Add the onion, carrot, celery and garlic and cook, stirring, for 5 minutes or until the vegetables have softened.

2 Add the ground beef to the pan (there is no need to add more oil), breaking it up into smaller pieces with a wooden spoon. Cook for 10 minutes or until the meat has browned.

3 Stir in the tomatoes, bay leaf, oregano, sugar and salt and pepper, then pour in the red wine, if using. Bring to the boil and stir well, then reduce the heat to low, cover, and cook for 20–25 minutes, until thickened. Stir the sauce from time to time.

4 While the sauce is cooking, bring a large pan of water to the boil. Add the tablespoon of salt, then add the pasta and cook according to the instructions on the packet, until the pasta is tender but still firm to the bite, stirring from time to time.

5 Drain the spaghetti in a colander. Remove the bay leaf from the sauce. Serve the pasta in a large shallow bowl with the sauce poured over and sprinkled with Parmesan.

Note: No wonder this Italian dish has become popular all over the world. It's easy to make, tastes delicious and it isn't expensive. Make sure you cook the spaghetti in plenty of boiling water and if you like, add a few drops of olive oil, help stop the pasta sticking together.

Serves 4

Veal Schnitzel with Glazed Apricots

Ingredients

4 veal steaks, thinly cut
1/2 cup all-purpose flour, seasoned with salt and pepper
2 eggs, lightly beaten
1 cup dry breadcrumbs
1 tbsp butter
1 tbsp oil

Glazed Apricots
16 apricots
1 cup water
1/2 cup brown sugar
1 tsp ground ginger
1 1/2 in/4 cm strip lemon zest
2 tbsp lemon juice

Method

1 Pound the steaks out thinly between 2 sheets of plastic wrap. Dip in the seasoned flour, then dip in the egg to coat. Spread half the breadcrumbs on kitchen paper, place the steaks on top and cover with the remaining crumbs. Press down well with the palm of your hand to firmly attach the crumbs. Place in a single layer on a tray. Cover and refrigerate for 30 minutes or more.

2 Place all the glazed apricot ingredients in a saucepan. Bring to the boil, turn down the heat and simmer for 5 minutes. Remove the apricots from the liquid with a slotted spoon and set aside. Boil liquid in the saucepan until reduced to a syrup.

3 Heat oil the and butter in a large fry pan. When hot, add 2 schnitzels and cook for about 2 minutes on each side; turn with tongs. Remove and cook the other 2 schnitzels. Drain on kitchen paper.

4 Serve on heated plates. Place 4 glazed apricots down the center of each schnitzel. Spoon the syrup on top. Serve immediately with vegetable accompaniments.

Serves 4

Lamb was the first meat to grace the table of mankind. It wins in the popularity stakes still, for it is a fine- to medium- grained meat with a velvety texture and a delightfully sweet flavor.

Lamb

Lamb Appetizers, Soups, Snacks, & Salads

Spicy Lamb Kebabs

Ingredients

½ **cup olive oil**

½ **cup of finely diced onion**

juice of 2 lemons

5 cloves of garlic, minced

1 tbsp fresh chopped cilantro

3 tsp ground cumin

2 tsp crumbled bay leaves

2 tsp paprika

½ **tsp ground turmeric**

2 lb/1 kg lamb, trimmed and cubed

1 large onion, cut into 1 in/2½ cm pieces

3 medium green bell pepper, cut into 1 in/2½ cm pieces

Method

1 Combine the oil, diced onion, lemon juice, garlic, cilantro, cumin bay leaves, paprika and tumeric. Mix well.

2 Place the lamb pieces with the marinade into a sealable container (a large zip-lock bag works best). Toss and refrigerate for 2–24 hours. The longer you marinade the more flavor the meat will gain.

3 Preheat the grill. Thread the lamb, onion and pepper pieces onto skewers, intermixing the pieces. Place the kebabs on the hot grill and cook for about 7–8 minutes, uncovered. Turn to cook each of the 4 sides for the same amount of time. Remove when cooked to your liking and serve with rice.

Serves 4

Middle-Eastern Spinach and Meatball Soup

Ingredients

2 tbsp olive oil

2 large leeks, washed and sliced

1 tbsp turmeric

1 tbsp cinnamon

4 oz/120 g yellow split peas

6 cups vegetable bouillon or water

1 lb/500 g spinach, washed and chopped

14 oz/400 g potatoes, peeled and diced

4 tbsp rice flour

juice of 2 lemons

salt and ground pepper, to taste

3 tbsp yogurt

oil for frying

4 shallots, sliced

10 mint leaves, finely sliced

Meatballs

1 large brown onion, finely minced

1/2 lb/250 g ground lamb

2 cloves garlic, minced

Method

1 Heat the olive oil and add the well-washed and sliced leeks to the saucepan, sautéing until they are golden. Add the turmeric and cinnamon and continue stirring and cooking until the mixture is fragrant (about 2 minutes). Add the yellow peas and bouillon or water and bring the mixture to the boil. Simmer for 30 minutes.

2 Meanwhile, make the meatballs. Mix together the minced onion, lamb, garlic and lots of salt and pepper to taste, then shape the meat mixture into walnut-sized balls. Drop the meatballs into the soup and simmer for 10 minutes. Add the well-washed and chopped spinach and potato cubes and continue simmering for 10 minutes more.

3 Mix the rice flour with a little water and the lemon juice and whisk until smooth, then drizzle this mixture into the soup, stirring, until it has all been added. Add salt and freshly ground black pepper to taste and simmer for 10 minutes more.

4 Finally, stir in the yogurt (do not allow the soup to boil). Heat a little extra oil then fry the shallot slices until crisp and deep golden brown. Garnish the soup with the fried shallots and the finely sliced mint leaves.

Serves 4

Moroccan Harira

Ingredients

2 tbsp butter
1½ tsp cinnamon
1 tsp ground ginger
1 tsp ground turmeric
1 tsp ground paprika
½ tsp ground black pepper
pinch of saffron threads
1 lb/500 g lamb fillets or shoulder, cut into cubes
1 large onion, finely chopped
⅓ cup chopped Italian parsley
⅓ cup chopped cilantro
14 oz/400 g chopped canned tomatoes
5–6 cups water
4 oz/125 g chickpeas, washed, picked over and soaked overnight
4 oz/125 g lentils, washed and picked over
2 tbsp lemon juice
salt, to taste
lemon slices and extra chopped parsley to serve (optional)

Method

1 In a large saucepan, melt the butter and stir in the cinnamon, ginger, turmeric, paprika, pepper and saffron threads. Cook slowly for 2 minutes to release their wonderful fragrances.

2 Add the cubed lamb, onion, parsley and cilantro and cook, stirring, until the lamb is brown and the onions are soft (about 15 minutes). Add the tomatoes and cook a further 5 minutes. Add the water and chickpeas and heat to boiling point. Simmer for 1 hour, partially covered.

3 Add the lentils and cook a further 45 minutes until the lentils are soft. Add the lemon juice and salt and cook for a further 5 minutes. Serve with lemon slices and extra parsley if desired.

Serves 4

Turkish Lamb Boreklers

Ingredients

1 tbsp butter
1 onion, very finely chopped
1 tsp fresh thyme leaves
1/2 lb/250 g lamb, ground
1 cup Italian parsley, chopped
2 tbsp currants, soaked in water for 10 minutes
2 tbsp pine nuts, toasted
3 tbsp roasted red bell pepper, finely chopped
salt and pepper, to taste
12 sheets of filo pastry
3 1/2 oz/100 g butter, melted

Tzatziki Dipping Sauce
1 cup Greek yogurt
4 tbsp fresh lemon juice
2 cloves garlic, minced
2 tbsp Italian parsley
3 tbsp olive oil
4 scallions, very finely chopped
salt and pepper, to taste

Method

1 Preheat an oven to 450°F/230°C/Gas Mark 8. Melt the butter in a heavy frypan, add the onion and thyme leaves, and sauté until golden (about 5 minutes). Add the ground lamb and sauté until the lamb is thoroughly cooked (about 5 minutes). Remove from the heat and add the parsley, currants, pine nuts, red pepper pieces and salt and pepper to taste. Stir well, then allow to cool.

2 To make the tzatziki dipping sauce, mix all the ingredients together in a bowl with a whisk (or in a blender) and stir until smooth. Refrigerate until ready to serve.

3 Lie one sheet of filo pastry on a clean work-surface and sparingly brush with melted butter. Place two more sheets on top, buttering between each one. (Keep the remaining sheets under a damp cloth or in plastic wrap.) Cut the filo stack into three rectangles and place a heaped tablespoon of filling near the short edge of each, remembering to leave a generous border on both sides. Fold the bottom edge of the pastry over the filling and roll up, folding in the sides of the pastry as you continue to roll up the pastry to form cigar shapes. Make sure there is no excess air trapped in the pastry. Repeat with the remaining pastry and filling the until all the ingredients are used.

4 Brush each pastry with melted butter (or oil) and place on a baking tray. Bake in a preheated oven at 450°F/230°C/Gas Mark 8 for 10–15 minutes, or until golden. Serve a pile of boreklers with the tzaziki sauce.

Makes 12 small pastries

Moroccan Lamb Pizza

Ingredients

- 1 tbsp sunflower oil
- 1 red onion, finely chopped
- 1 clove garlic, crushed
- 1/2 lb/225 g lean ground lamb
- 1/2 cup canned crushed tomatoes
- 1 tsp ground cumin
- 1 tsp ground coriander
- 1/2 tsp cinnamon
- 1 tbsp chopped fresh cilantro
- 1 tbsp lemon juice
- 4 single-serve pizza bases
- 2 tbsp pine nuts, toasted
- 4 oz/125 g reduced-fat mozzarella cheese, grated
- 1 cup fresh mint leaves
- 1 cup fresh Italian parsley
- cracked black pepper
- 2 tbsp mango relish

Raita Yogurt Relish

- 1 cup reduced-fat natural yogurt
- 1 Lebanese cucumber, grated
- 1 clove garlic, crushed
- 1 tbsp fresh mint, chopped

Method

1 Heat the oil in a frypan, add the onion and clove of crushed garlic and cook over a medium heat for 1 minute. Add the lamb and cook until the lamb is browned, breaking the meat up with a fork. Drain any excess oil from the pan. Add the tomatoes, cumin, ground cilantro and cinnamon and cook for 5 minutes. Stir in the fresh cilantro and 2 teaspoons lemon juice.

2 Preheat the oven to 400°F/200°C/Gas Mark 6. Spread the lamb topping over the pizza bases and sprinkle with the pine nuts and mozzarella. Bake for 10 minutes or until the cheese has melted and the pizzas are heated through.

3 To make the raita, mix the yogurt, grated cucumber, crushed clove of garlic and chopped mint in a bowl.

4 Toss the mint and parsley leaves in the remaining lemon juice and season with pepper. Serve the pizzas topped with the herb leaves, raita and relish.

Serves 4

Low-Fat Mini Meatballs

Ingredients
1 2/3 lb/750 g lean ground lamb
1 tsp chopped ginger
1 bunch fresh chives, chopped
1/2 bunch fresh cilantro, chopped
1 egg
sprinkle garlic steak seasoning
dry breadcrumbs

Method
1 Mix all the ingredients except the breadcrumbs in a bowl.

2 Using a dessertspoon, form small balls. Coat the meatballs with the dry breadcrumbs.

3 Dry-fry the meat balls in a pre-heated electric frying pan lined with baking paper. (Crumbed meatballs to be placed on top of the paper). Cook on high for 8–10 minutes, turning every couple of minutes. Serve on a bed of iceberg lettuce.

Serves 4

Lamb and Lemon Kebabs

Ingredients
1/4 cup olive oil
2 cloves garlic, crushed
2 tsp ground cumin
1 tsp paprika
2 1/2 fl oz/75 mL lemon juice
1 tsp finely grated lemon zest
1/4 cup coconut cream
1 1/2 lb/750 g lean lamb, cut into 3/4 in/2 cm cubes
1 tbsp chopped fresh parsley
1 cup plain low-fat yogurt
1 tbsp chopped fresh mint

Method
1 Combine the oil, garlic, cumin, paprika, lemon juice, lemon zest, and coconut cream in a large non-metallic bowl. Add the lamb, mix well, cover, and marinate in the refrigerator for at least 6 hours and up to 24 hours.

2 Preheat the broiler. Thread the lamb onto skewers; broil under moderate heat for 3 minutes on each side or until cooked. Sprinkle with parsley. Combine the yogurt and mint and serve with the kebabs.

Serves 8

Low-Fat Mini Meatballs

Lamb Mains

Lamb Cutlets with Olives

Ingredients

1 tbsp olive oil

2 cloves garlic, minced

8–12 lamb cutlets, depending on size

5 fl oz/150 mL white wine

5 fl oz/150 mL beef bouillon

2 tbsp tomato paste

2 sprigs rosemary, roughly chopped

1/3 cup black olives

freshly ground black pepper, to taste

Method

1 Preheat the oven to 350°F/180°C/Gas Mark 4.

2 Heat the oil in a large frying pan, add the garlic and lamb cutlets, and brown, on medium heat for 2–3 minutes on each side.

3 Add the wine and cook for 2 minutes. Mix the tomato paste with the beef bouillon and add to the lamb cutlets. Add the rosemary, black olives and pepper.

4 Transfer the lamb to a casserole dish and bake, for 30–40 minutes.

Serves 4

Irish Stew

Ingredients

8 best neck lamb chops
3 large old potatoes, peeled and sliced into thick slices
2 large carrots, sliced
1/2 cup chopped fresh parsley
salt and pepper, to taste
2 tbsp all-purpose flour
a little milk (optional)

Method

1 Layer the chops, potatoes, carrots, and parsley in a casserole dish. Season, to taste, and cover with boiling water. Put the lid on the casserole and cook oven for 1 1/2 hours.

2 Thicken the stew by mixing the flour with a little sauce from the stew. Stir into the stew and place back into the oven for a further 10 minutes.

3 For a creamy gravy, replace some of the liquid from the stew with a little milk after cooking.

Serves 4

Cilantro Shanks

Ingredients

1 tbsp olive oil
4 lamb shanks
1 onion, sliced
1 carrot, sliced
14 oz/400 g canned tomatoes, undrained and mashed
1 tsp ground allspice
1/2 tsp ground cumin
1/2 tsp ground cilantro
2 tsp paprika
1 tsp finely grated lemon zest
1 cup beef bouillon
2 tbsp lemon juice
2 tbsp chopped fresh cilantro

Method

1 Heat the oil in a large frying pan and cook the shanks over a high heat for 5 minutes or until brown on all sides. Transfer to a large flameproof casserole dish.

2 Add the onion and carrot to the pan and cook for 5 minutes or until the onion is soft. Transfer to the casserole dish. Stir in the tomatoes, allspice, cumin, ground cilantro, paprika, lemon zest and bouillon, then cover and bake, at 350°F/180°C/Gas Mark 4 for 1 1/2–2 hours or until the meat is tender.

3 Remove the shanks from the casserole, stir in the lemon juice and cook over a high heat until the sauce reduces and thickens. Return the shanks to the sauce and sprinkle with the fresh cilantro.

Serves 4

Irish Stew

Macaroni with Lamb Ragu

Ingredients

2 tbsp olive oil
2 oz/55 g butter
1 stick celery, finely chopped
1 onion, finely chopped
1 small carrot, finely chopped
12 oz/350 g lean ground lamb
1 cup whole milk
salt and black pepper
12 oz/350 g dried short-cut macaroni
2 tbsp chopped fresh mint to garnish
freshly grated Parmesan cheese to serve

Method

1 Heat the oil and butter in a large heavy-based frying pan and gently fry the celery, onion, and carrot for 5–7 minutes, until softened. Add the lamb and cook, stirring, for 5–6 minutes, until the meat has browned, then season.

2 Reduce the heat to very low and stir in the milk 2–3 tablespoons at a time, ensuring that each addition is absorbed before adding the next. This should take 30 minutes, by which time the vegetables will be tender and the meat cooked. Season with salt and pepper.

3 Cook the pasta in plenty of boiling salted water, until tender but still firm to the bite, then drain. Mix in 4–5 tablespoons of the sauce, then divide among 4 warmed bowls and spoon over the rest of the sauce. Garnish with mint and serve the Parmesan separately.

Note: This pasta's simple meaty sauce is given a lovely richness using a traditional Sardinian technique. While it is cooking, milk is added, little by little, until it has all been absorbed.

Serves 4

Indian Meatballs in Tomato Sauce

Ingredients

- **1 lb/500 g ground lamb**
- **5 tbsp plain yogurt**
- **2 in/5 cm piece fresh root ginger, finely chopped**
- **1 green chili, deseeded and finely chopped**
- **3 tbsp chopped fresh cilantro**
- **2 tsp ground cumin**
- **2 tsp ground cilantro**
- salt and black pepper
- **2 tbsp vegetable oil**
- **1 onion, chopped**
- **2 cloves garlic, chopped**
- **1/2 tsp turmeric**
- **1 tsp garam masala**
- **14 oz/400 g can chopped tomatoes**

Method

1 Mix together the lamb, 1 tablespoon of the yogurt, the ginger, chili, 2 tablespoons of the chopped cilantro, the cumin, and ground cilantro and season. Shape the mixture into 16 balls.

2 Heat 1 tablespoon of the oil in a large saucepan, then fry the meatballs for 10 minutes, turning until browned (you may have to cook them in batches). Drain on paper towels and set aside.

3 Heat the remaining oil in the pan. Add the onion and garlic and fry for 5 minutes or until softened, stirring occasionally. Mix the turmeric and garam masala with 1 tablespoon of water, then add to the onion and garlic. Add the remaining yogurt, 1 tablespoon at a time, stirring well each time.

4 Add the tomatoes, meatballs and 1/2 cup pint of water to the mixture and bring to the boil. Partly cover the pan, reduce the heat and simmer for 30 minutes, stirring occasionally. Sprinkle over the rest of the cilantro to garnish.

Note: Serve these meatballs, or *koftas*, on their own as a snack, or with rice and the spicy tomato sauce as a main course.

Serves 4

Keema Curry

Ingredients

- 1 tbsp vegetable oil
- 1 onion, finely chopped
- 1 in/2½ cm piece fresh root ginger, grated
- 2 cloves garlic, crushed
- 1 lb/500 g lean ground lamb
- 2 tsp ground turmeric
- 1 tsp chili powder
- 1 tbsp garam masala
- 3 tbsp tomato paste
- 2 cups lamb bouillon
- 4 oz/125 g frozen baby peas
- salt and black pepper
- 2 tbsp chopped fresh cilantro, plus extra leaves to garnish

Method

1 Heat the oil in a large heavy-based frying pan. Add the onion and ginger and cook over a low heat for 5 minutes or until softened. Add the garlic and ground lamb, breaking the ground lamb into pieces by pressing with the back of a wooden spoon. Cook for 10 minutes or until the lamb browns.

2 Pour off any excess fat from the pan. Add the turmeric, chili, garam masala and tomato paste, then stir-fry for 1–2 minutes. Add the bouillon and bring to the boil, stirring, then reduce the heat and simmer, uncovered, for 10 minutes or until slightly reduced.

3 Add the peas, then simmer for 5–10 minutes longer. Remove from the heat, stir in the cilantro and season. Garnish with the extra cilantro.

Note: This is a really easy way to turn ground lamb into a delicious spicy curry. It's best served the traditional way – with basmati rice, cucumber raita and mango relish.

Serves 4

Pesto-Crusted Racks of Lamb

Ingredients

4–6 racks of lamb, 3–4 cutlets on each

1 tsp crushed garlic

3 cups soft, white breadcrumbs

¼ cup pinenuts

3 tbsp fresh chopped basil

2 tbsp grated Romano or Parmesan cheese

1 tbsp lemon juice

1 small egg, lightly beaten

Method

1 Trim some of the fat from the racks, leaving a thin layer. Rub all over with a little crushed garlic. Mix the remaining ingredients together to form a damp mixture. Pack this mixture onto each rack, patting down well. Place the racks onto a flat tray, cover with plastic wrap and refrigerate.

2 Serve with basil tomatoes and bruschettes. Serves 2–3 cutlets per serve. Place the racks in pairs, back-to-back for support. Cover with the barbecue lid or hood and cook for 35–45 minutes. Remove from the barbecue, cover with foil and rest the meat for 5 minutes before serving.

3 For a kettle barbecue/hooded gas barbecue: Place the racks of lamb on oiled grill bars, over drip pan, in an upright position. (Not suitable for flat-top barbecue)

Lamb and Sweet Potato Stew

Ingredients

1 tbsp olive oil
12 lamb cutlets
3 cups lamb or chicken bouillon
2 onions, thinly sliced
1 1/2 lb/750 g sweet potatoes, cut into 1/4 in/1 cm thick slices
11 oz/300 g carrots, chopped
5 sticks celery, chopped
6–7 fresh sage leaves or 1 tsp dried sage
4–5 fresh thyme sprigs or 1 tsp dried thyme
salt and black pepper
3 tbsp pearl barley

Method

1 Preheat the oven to 350°F/180°C/Gas Mark 4. Heat the oil in a large, heavy-based frying pan and fry the cutlets for 1–2 minutes on each side to brown (you may have to do this in batches). Remove the cutlets, discard the oil and add a little bouillon to the pan. Bring to the boil, stirring and scraping the bottom of the pan, then bouillon the rest of the bouillon.

2 Place half the onions in a large ovenproof casserole dish. Top with one-third of the sweet potatoes, then add half the carrots and celery, and all the sage, thyme, and cutlets. Season, then sprinkle the barley over. Repeat the layering and top with the remaining sweet potatoes. Pour the bouillon over and cover.

3 Cook for 1 1/2 hours or until the lamb is tender, checking occasionally and adding more bouillon or water if the casserole is becoming too dry. Remove the lid and increase the oven heat to 450°F/230°C/Gas Mark 8. Cook for 8–10 minutes, until the potatoes have browned.

Serves 6

Lamb Fillets with Salsa Pilaf

Ingredients
2 lamb fillets (about 1 1/2 lb/750 g)
1/2 tsp crushed garlic
1 tbsp lemon juice
2 tsp olive oil
salt and pepper

Salsa Pilaf
1 1/2 cups uncooked rice
6 cups boiling water
2 oz/55 g pine nuts, toasted
10 oz/285 g jar tomato salsa
2 tbsp currants

Method

1 Trim the lamb fillets, removing the fine silver membrane. Place in a dish and add the garlic, lemon juice, oil, salt, and pepper. Cover and for stand 30 minutes.

2 Cook the rice in the boiling, salted water for about 15 minutes, until rice is tender. Drain well and keep hot. Heat a small saucepan, add the pine nuts and shake over the heat until they colour. Add the salsa and currants and heat through.

3 Heat the barbecue grill plate and oil lightly. Set at medium-high. Place the lamb on the grill and cook for 6–8 minutes, turning to cook on all sides. Cook longer for well done. Rest for 5 minutes before slicing in 1/2 in/1 cm slices.

4 Using a cup or mold, form a mound of rice on the plate. Pour the salsa over the rice and arrange the lamb slices at the base of the rice mound.

Serves 4–5

Roast Lamb with Beans and Tomatoes

Ingredients

1 lb/500 g dried haricot beans or fresh borlotti beans
2 large onions, quartered
bouquet garni
2 cloves garlic
1 tsp salt
a few peppercorns
1 leg of lamb
salt and freshly ground pepper
1 cup water
2 oz/55 g butter
4 scallions, chopped (or 1 small onion)
2 large ripe tomatoes, peeled and diced
2 tbsp chopped parsley

Method

1 Soak the beans overnight in water to cover and drain. Place in a large pan with fresh water to cover, add the onions, bouquet garni, 1 clove garlic, salt and peppercorns. Bring slowly to the boil, skim and cover. Cook gently for 1½–2 hours or until the beans are tender. If using fresh or frozen borlotti beans, do not soak but cook as for haricots; they will take ¾–1 hour.

2 Meanwhile, cut the excess fat from the lamb and season. Cut a few small incisions between the skin and flesh. Sliver the remaining garlic clove and insert into the slits in the lamb. Place the lamb on a rack. Put the water and half the butter in the dish. Bake in a preheated oven 375°F/190°C/Gas Mark 5 for 1¼ hours, basting every 15 minutes. The flesh should be still quite pink.

3 Melt the remaining butter in a pan 30 minutes before the lamb is due to finish cooking. Add the scallions and cook gently until softened. Add the tomatoes and drained beans and ½ cup of the lamb juice from the dish. Cover and simmer gently for a further 15 minutes.

4 Place the lamb on a serving platter and strain any juices from the dish into a sauceboat. Toss the beans with the parsley and serve separately. Oven temperature 375°F/190°C/Gas Mark 6.

Serves 6

Lamb Hotpot Cooked in Cider

Ingredients

2 tbsp olive oil

4 loin lamb chops

6 lamb kidneys, halved and skins and cores removed

1 onion, sliced

1½ lb/750 g potatoes, sliced

2 carrots, sliced

1 large leek, sliced

2 sticks celery, sliced

salt and black pepper

3 sprigs fresh marjoram or oregano

1¼ cups dry cider

Method

1 Preheat the oven to 350°F/180°C/Gas Mark 4. Heat 1 tablespoon of the oil in a large heavy-based frying pan. Add the chops and cook for 1–2 minutes on each side, until browned. Remove from the pan, then add the kidneys and cook for 30 seconds on each side or until lightly browned.

2 Arrange half the onion and potatoes in the base of a casserole dish. Top with the chops; add half the carrots, leek, and celery, and then the kidneys. Add the rest of the carrots, leek, and celery, seasoning each layer well. Finish with a layer of onions and potatoes, then tuck in the marjoram or oregano sprigs. Pour the cider over and brush the top with the remaining oil.

3 Cover and cook for 1½–2 hours, until the meat is tender. Remove the lid, place near the top of the oven and cook for 20–30 minutes, until brown.

Note: This slow-cooked hotpot produces meltingly tender meat. It's an ideal weekend lunch – once it's in the oven you can forget about it for a couple of hours.

Serves 4

South African Bobotie

Ingredients

- 1 tbsp vegetable oil
- 1 onion, finely chopped
- 2 thick slices of white bread, broken into pieces (crusts removed)
- 1 1/2 cups whole milk
- 1 lb/455 g lean ground lamb
- 2 tbsp mild or hot curry paste
- 2 cloves garlic, crushed
- salt and black pepper
- juice of 1/2 lemon
- 3 oz/85 g ready-to-eat dried apricots, chopped, or raisins
- 2 oz/55 g flaked almonds
- 2 medium eggs, beaten

Method

1 Preheat the oven to 350°F/180°C/Gas Mark 4. Heat the oil in a large heavy-based frying pan, add the onion and fry for 5 minutes to soften. Place the bread in a bowl with the milk and leave to soak.

2 Meanwhile, add the ground lamb to the pan and cook for 10 minutes or until browned, breaking the mince up with a wooden spoon. Add the curry paste, garlic, and seasoning and cook for 5 minutes. Add the lemon juice, apricots or raisins, and half of the almonds to the pan and mix well.

3 Lift the bread out of the milk and squeeze gently to remove some of the liquid. Reserve the milk and add the bread to the pan. Transfer the lamb mixture to an ovenproof dish, discarding any excess fat. Whisk the eggs into the remaining milk and season. Pour over the lamb mixture and sprinkle with the remaining almonds. Cook for 30 minutes or until the top has set and is golden.

Note: This is South Africa's answer to shepherd's pie. Sweet and spicy ground lamb is hidden under a golden topping, scattered with flaked almonds. Serve with a green salad.

Serves 4

Lamb Racks with Broad Bean and Pea Purée

Ingredients

4 x 4 cutlet racks of lamb (about 1 1/2 lb/750 g)
2 cloves garlic, sliced
2 sprigs fresh rosemary, torn
1/2 cup mint jelly
2 tbsp wholegrain mustard
2 tbsp balsamic vinegar

Broad Bean and Pea Purée
1 lb/500 g fresh or frozen broad beans, thawed and peeled
1 cup frozen mint peas
1/2 cup reduced-salt chicken bouillon

Method

1 Preheat the oven to 400°F/200°C/Gas Mark 6. Trim any excess fat from the rack and any sinew away from the bones using a small sharp knife. Cut small slits in the lamb and put slices of garlic and torn sprigs of rosemary into each slit.

2 Put the mint jelly, mustard, and balsamic vinegar into a small saucepan and bring to the boil. Brush the lamb racks with the glaze and put into a baking dish.

3 Roast the racks for 35–40 minutes for medium rare. Allow to stand for 5 minutes before cutting into cutlets.

4 To make the Broad Bean and Pea Purée. While the lamb roasts, put the broad beans, peas and bouillon in a pot, bring to the boil then reduce the heat and simmer until the broad beans are soft and most of the liquid is absorbed. Mash until very smooth or put in a food processor and blend until smooth.

5 Serve the cutlets on a mound of broad bean purée, drizzle with the warmed glaze and serve with steamed or roasted baby potatoes.

Serves 4

Roasted Leg of Lamb with Vegetables

Ingredients

4½ lb/2 kg leg of lamb
2 cloves garlic, cut into slivers
1–2 fresh rosemary sprigs, cut into small pieces
salt and black pepper
1 lb/500 g parsnips, chopped
14 oz/400 g carrots, chopped
6 heads chicory, cut into quarters, lengthways
1¼ cups red or white wine
2 tbsp red wine vinegar

Method

1 Preheat the oven to 350°F/180°C/Gas Mark 4. Make several incisions in the leg of lamb, using a sharp knife. Push the garlic slivers and pieces of rosemary into the incisions. Season the lamb well.

2 Arrange the vegetables in a large roasting tin and place the lamb on top. Pour in the wine and vinegar and roast for 2–2½ hours, until the lamb is tender, basting the lamb and turning the vegetables in the cooking juices every 30 minutes. Add a little more wine or water if necessary.

3 Transfer the lamb to a plate, reserving the cooking juices, then cover with foil and rest for 15 minutes. Carve the lamb and serve with the vegetables, with the cooking juices drizzled over.

Note: Garlic, rosemary and wine go beautifully with lamb and using all three guarantees an irresistible dish. Roasted chicory, carrots and parsnips complete the meal.

Serves 6

Barbecued Leg of Lamb in Paper

Ingredients

4 1/2 lb/2 kg leg of lamb

2 tsp salt

1 tsp pepper

1/2 cup lemon juice

2 tbsp freshy crushed garlic

Romano or Parmesan cheese cut into 8 x 1/5 in/1/2 cm cubes

5 1/2 oz/165 g jar sun-dried tomato pesto

Method

1 Wash the lamb and pat dry. Make about 8 incisions on each side of the lamb with the point of a small knife. Place the lamb in a non-corrosive dish, rub all over with salt and pepper, and pour the lemon juice over, allowing the juice to enter the incisions. Stand for 30 minutes. Push a 1/2 teaspoon of crushed garlic into each incision, followed by a cheese cube. Rub all over with tomato pesto. Wrap the lamb in 2 sheets of oiled waxed paper and then wrap into a parcel with brown paper. Tie with kitchen string.

2 Prepare kettle or gas hooded barbecue for indirect heat on medium-high. Place the lamb parcel onto oiled grill bars over the drip tray and cook, over indirect heat, for 2 hours. Turn the lamb after 1 hour. When cooked, remove from the barbecue and rest for 20 minutes before removing from the paper and carving. Take care when opening the parcel that any juices are collected in a bowl. Reheat the juices and serve with the carved meat. Serve with a mild mustard, a green salad and garlic bread

Serves 6–8

105

Shepherd's Pie

Ingredients

1 1/2 lb/675 g potatoes, peeled and cut into even-sized chunks
salt and black pepper
2 tbsp vegetable oil
1 medium onion, peeled and chopped
1 stick celery, diced
1 medium carrot, peeled and diced
1 lb/500 g ground lamb
1 tbsp tomato paste
2 tbsp Worcestershire sauce
6 fl oz/175 mL lamb bouillon made with 1/2 a bouillon cube
1 oz/30 g butter
2 fl oz/55 mL whole milk

Method

1 Put the potatoes into a saucepan, cover with cold water and add 1/2 teaspoon of salt. Boil for 20 minutes or until tender.

2 Meanwhile, preheat the oven to 400°F/200°C/Gas Mark 6. Heat the oil in a large heavy-based frying pan over a medium heat, then fry the onion, celery, and carrot for 2–3 minutes, until softened.

3 Add the ground lamb to the pan, breaking it up with the back of a wooden spoon. Cook for 5 minutes or until browned, stirring all the time. Stir in the tomato paste and Worcestershire sauce, mixing well. Cook for 2 minutes. Add the bouillon, stir, season to taste with salt and black pepper, then simmer for 5 minutes.

4 Meanwhile, drain the potatoes and return them to the pan. Add the butter and milk, then mash with a potato masher or fork until smooth.

5 Spoon the ground lamb mixture into a deep ovenproof dish, about 15 cm x 23 cm/6 in x 9 in in size. Top with the mashed potatoes, spreading them evenly and fluffing up the surface with a fork. Cook for 20 minutes or until the top is golden brown. Or try this ...

6 Peel and chop a clove of garlic and add it to the onions as they cook, or stir in 1 teaspoon of dried oregano. Or, for a crispy topping, sprinkle a handful of grated Cheddar over the mashed potato before you put the dish in the oven.

Note: There's something very comforting about shepherd's pie with its rich, meaty filling and creamy potato topping. You can assemble the pie up to a day in advance, as long as you leave it to cool, then keep it in the refrigerator. When you reheat it, increase the final cooking time by 10 minutes, to make absolutely sure that it's heated through.

Serves 4

107

Pork is a delicately flavored meat which lends itself to interesting flavor combinations. The flesh is finely grained with little connective tissue which means that all cuts are tender and quick and easy to cook.

Pork

Pork Appetizers, Snacks, & Salads

Thai Pork Sausage Rolls

Ingredients

- 1 lb/500 g lean ground pork
- 1 tsp ground cumin
- 1 tsp ground cilantro
- 2 tbsp sweet chili sauce
- 2 tbsp chopped fresh cilantro
- 1 cup fresh breadcrumbs
- 4 sheets frozen canola puff pastry, thawed and halved lengthwise
- 2 tbsp low- or reduced-fat milk

Method

1 Preheat oven to 400°F/200°C/Gas Mark 6.

2 Put the ground pork, cumin, ground cilantro, sweet chili sauce, fresh cilantro, and breadcrumbs in a bowl and mix to combine.

3 Spread one quarter of the mixture along one edge of one thawed sheet of pastry and roll up to conceal the filling. Repeat with the remaining filling and pastry sheets. Cut each roll into 6 bite sized sausage rolls and place the rolls seam-side down on 2 baking trays lined with waxed paper.

4 Lightly brush the rolls with milk and bake for 20 minutes or until the pastry is crisp and golden and the filling is cooked through.

5 Serve hot with tomato or sweet chili sauce.

Makes 24

Lemon Grass Pork Skewers

Ingredients

1 lb 2 oz/510 g pork leg steak or schnitzel, or scotch steak

Marinade
3 cloves garlic, crushed
2 tbsp fresh lemon grass, chopped
1/4 cup cilantro stalks, chopped
1 tbsp brown sugar
1/2 tsp ground cilantro
1/4 tsp white pepper
2 tbsp salt-reduced soy sauce
2 tbsp fish sauce
2 tbsp sesame oil
2 1/2 fl oz/75 mL cold water
bottled sweet chili sauce

Method

1 Cut approximately 16 wooden skewers in half and soak in water. Mix the marinade ingredients together.

2 Cut the pork into thin strips, thread 1 or 2 strips onto each skewer and marinate for 20 minutes or longer.

3 Heat a non-stick frying pan, barbecue plate or grill over a medium-hot heat.

4 Add oil and pan-fry for about 1–2 minutes on each side or until medium done. Avoid overcooking.

5 Serve with sweet chili sauce.

Makes about 32 skewers

Serves 4

Tandoori Pork and Mango Pockets

Ingredients

4 lean pork loin or leg steaks
1/4 cup Tandoori Marinade (see below)
16 oz/455 g can mango slices
4 1/2 oz/125 g plain yogurt
1 1/2 tbsp freshly chopped cilantro
2 tsp vegetable oil
4 pita (pocket) bread
1 medium red onion, thinly sliced
1 oz/30 g baby argula leaves

Tandoori Marinade

1 tbsp grated fresh ginger
2 tsp cilantro seeds, toasted
2 tsps fresh rosemary leaves
1 tsp grated lemon zest
1/2 tsp ground cardamom
1/2 tsp ground cumin
1/4 tsp crushed black peppercorns
1/4 tsp chili sauce or powder
1/2 cup low-fat plain yogurt
1 tbsp lemon juice

Method

1 To make the Tandooro Marinade, place the ginger, cilantro seeds, rosemary, lemon zest, cardamom, cumin, black peppercorns, chili sauce, yogurt, and lemon juice in a bowl. Mix to combine.

2 Combine the pork and Tandoori Marinade in a bowl and coat well. Cover and allow to marinate for 30 minutes.

3 Drain the mango slices well in a strainer. Combine the yogurt and cilantro, cover and place in the refrigerator.

4 Heat the oil on a hot barbecue plate or grill and cook the pork for 3–4 minutes on each side, depending on thickness. Allow pork to rest for the a few minutes before slicing into pieces about 1/2 in/1 cm wide.

5 Cut the pita bread in half then spread each half inside with the cilantro yogurt. Assemble the pockets with the pork and mango slices, onion and argula.

Serves 4

Pork San Choy Bau

Ingredients

2 tsp peanut oil

1 small onion, finely chopped

1 tbsp thinly shredded ginger

1 lb 2 oz/510 g lean ground pork

2 tbsp salt-reduced soy sauce

2 tbsp hoisin sauce

3 tsp sweet chili sauce

3 oz/85 g sliced green scallions

1 small cucumber, halved and peeled into long thin strips

8 small iceberg lettuce leaves

Method

1 Heat the oil in a frying pan or wok over a medium-high heat; add the onion and ginger and cook for 1 minute, stirring continuously.

2 Add the pork, stir to combine, and cook for 4 minutes. Stir in the soy, hoisin and chili sauces and cook for 10 minutes, stirring occasionally. Add the scallions.

3 To serve, place a few strips of cucumber in each lettuce leaf and top with cooked pork. Roll each lettuce leaf to encase the filling.

Serves 4

Honeyed Spare Ribs

Ingredients

16 pork spare ribs, trimmed of visible fat

1 1/2 cups rice wine vinegar

1/2 cup soy sauce

1/2 cup honey

4 small fresh red chilies, seeds removed and chopped

2 scallions, chopped

4 cloves garlic, crushed

1 tbsp grated fresh ginger

2 onions, chopped

1 cup chicken bouillon

2 tbsp lemon juice

2 tbsp chopped fresh parsley

2 oz/55 g butter, melted

Method

1 Place the spare ribs in a large non-corrosive dish. Place the vinegar, soy sauce, honey, chilies, scallions, garlic, and ginger in a bowl and mix to combine. Pour over the spare ribs, cover, and refrigerate for at least 4 hours or overnight.

2 Drain the ribs and reserve the marinade. Cook the ribs on a preheated barbecue, brushing occasionally with some of the reserved marinade, for 15–20 minutes or until golden and tender.

3 To make the sauce, place the remaining reserved bouillon, onions, bouillon, lemon juice, and parsley in a saucepan. Bring to the boil, reduce the heat and cook, uncovered, for 15 minutes or until the sauce is reduced by half. Place the sauce in a food processor or blender and, with the machine running, pour in the hot melted butter and process to combine. Pour the sauce over the hot ribs or pass around separately.

Serves 8

Pork San Choy Bau

Pork and Mushroom Kebabs with Black Olives

Ingredients

1 clove garlic, finely chopped
2 tbsp finely chopped fresh Italian parsley
1 tbsp finely chopped pitted black olives
finely grated zest and juice of 1 fresh lime
2 fl oz/55 mL olive oil
cracked black pepper
1 lb/455 g lean diced pork pieces (³/₄ in/2 cm cubes)
7 oz/200 g Swiss brown mushrooms, cut into pieces

Method

1 Soak 8 wooden skewers in water for 1–2 hours. Combine garlic, parsley, olives, lime zest and juice the oil, and pepper to taste.

2 Thread the pork and mushrooms onto the skewers, about the 3 pieces of mushroom and pork per kebab.

3 Cook on a lightly oiled barbecue or grill over a medium-high heat for 5–6 minutes (turn 2–3 times) or until the juices run pink to clear when pierced with a skewer. Brush the kebabs with the seasoned oil twice during cooking.

4 Spoon the remaining black olive garlic oil over the kebabs and serve.

5 Serve with potato wedges and salad.

Serves 4

119

Ground Pork and Date Burgers

Ingredients

1 lb/455 g lean ground pork
¼ cup finely chopped fresh dates
1 tsp ground cardamom
¼ tsp ground cloves
½ tsp freshly grated ginger
finely grated zest and juice of 1 fresh lime
¼ cup freshly chopped mint
1 egg, lightly beaten
1 medium eggplant
2 fl oz/55 mL olive oil
8 pieces bought roasted red bell pepper
baby arugula leaves
onion relish (optional)

Method

1 Combine the ground pork, dates, cardamom, cloves, ginger and juice lime zest, mint, and egg. Mix together well. Shape the mixture into 8 small burgers; put onto a plate. Cover and chill for 30 minutes.

2 Cut the eggplant into ½ in/1 cm thick slices. Lightly brush with 2 tbsp of oil during cooking. Cook and grill for 10 minutes or until lightly golden.

3 Meanwhile, heat the a remaining oil in a frying pan over medium-low heat and cook the burgers for 12–14 minutes, or until the juices run clear and hot. Turn 2–3 times during cooking.

4 Serve the pork burgers on the eggplant accompanied by the baby arugula leaves, and relish.

Serves 4

Pork Pâté

Ingredients
4 long strips bacon, rind removed
1 1/2 lb/680 g best-quality ground pork
2 eggs, lightly beaten
1 tsp dried tarragon
a good pinch each of ground cloves, nutmeg, and ginger
1 tsp salt
a good grinding of black pepper
1/2 cup brandy

Luting Paste
7 oz/200 g all-purpose flour
approximately 1 cup water

Method

1 Arrange the bacon evenly on the base and sides of a 3 1/2-cup terrine or other ovenproof dish, letting the ends overhang.

2 With a wooden spoon, mix together the ground pork, eggs, tarragon, spices, salt, and pepper. Beat until very well combined. (This may be done in a food processor.)

3 Preheat the oven to 350°F/180°C/Gas Mark 4. Warm the brandy, ignite, and add to the pork mixture once the flames subside. Mix well. Fill the lined terrine with this mixture and cross over the ends of the bacon decoratively.

4 Make the Luting Paste; put the flour into a bowl and make a well in the center. Using your fingers, gradually mix the water into the flour to obtain a soft paste, just firm enough to shape (do not beat the mixture). Turn onto a floured board and roll into a rope the length of the perimeter of your terrine.

5 Cover the terrine with a piece of foil, then a lid, and seal the lid to the dish with the Luting Paste. Bake for 1–1 1/2 hours. For best results, stand the dish in a pan of boiling water.

6 Remove from the oven, break away and discard the luting, and take off the lid. Place a plate directly on top of the pâté and a weight on the plate. (If using an oblong terrine, use a piece of wood cut to fit and covered with foil instead of a plate.) Leave to cool completely, then top with a fresh piece of foil. Chill before serving with crisp salad vegetables such as radishes, scallions, or celery, and cornichons or other pickles.

Serves 4

Warm Vegetable Salad with Serrano Ham

Ingredients
salt and black pepper
2 leeks, white parts only, sliced
7 oz/200 g shelled broad beans or garden peas
5 oz/145 g snow peas
3 tbsp olive oil
1 clove garlic, thinly sliced
3 scallions, cut into 2 in/5 cm lengths
3 oz/85 g baby spinach
3 slices Serrano ham, cut into thin slices
2 large open mushrooms, very thinly sliced
few drops of lemon juice
Parmesan cheese to serve (optional)

Method

1 Bring a large saucepan of lightly salted water to the boil. Add the leeks, broad beans or peas and cook for 2 minutes, then add the snowpeas and stir for a few seconds. Drain and set aside.

2 Add 2 tablespoons of oil to the pan, then add the garlic and scallions. Stir for a minute to soften slightly, then tip in the spinach and stir until it starts to wilt. Add the cooked vegetables to the pan with the remaining oil. Lightly season and fry for 2 minutes to heat through.

3 Add the ham to the pan and heat through for 1–2 minutes. Arrange the mixture on a serving plate. Scatter the mushrooms over and sprinkle with lemon juice. Shave over the Parmesan, if using, and season with black pepper.

Note: Salty Serrano ham works brilliantly in this warm salad of fresh young vegetables. Remove the skins of a few broad beans to reveal their pretty bright green color.

Serves 6

Ham and Mushroom Filo Tartlets

Ingredients

cooking oil spray

1 tbsp light olive oil

4 oz/100 g button mushrooms, sliced

6 scallions, thinly sliced

1 clove garlic, crushed

2 oz/55 g reduced-fat Cheddar cheese, grated

7 oz/200 g reduced fat ricotta

2 eggs

1/2 tsp nutmeg

black pepper, to taste

6 slices reduced-fat ham

4 sheets of filo pastry

Method

1 Preheat the oven to 350°F/180°C/Gas Mark 4. Spray 8 large 1 cup capacity muffin tins with cooking oil spray.

2 Heat oil in a fry pan and cook the mushrooms, scallions and garlic over a high heat for 3 minutes or until the mushrooms are browned. Cool slightly.

3 Put the mushrooms in a bowl, add the Cheddar, ricotta, eggs, and nutmeg and season with black pepper. Cut the ham into thin strips and fold into the mixture.

4 Lay the sheets of filo on top of each other, cut in half lengthwise then cut even strip into 4 even pieces. Spray 4 pieces with cooking spray and layer unevenly in each muffin tin; repeat with the remaining pieces.

5 Spoon the filling into the cases. Bake for 20–25 minutes until lightly golden. Leave for a few minutes before gently easing out and serve with a crisp green salad.

Makes 8

Warm Lima Bean and Prosciutto Salad with Arugula

Ingredients

1 lb/500 g dried lima beans
2 tbsp olive oil
½ tsp dried chili flakes
3 cloves garlic, minced
3½ oz/100 g prosciutto, roughly chopped
salt and freshly ground pepper
10 basil leaves, torn
2 handfuls of arugula leaves

Method

1 Place the lima beans in a large bowl of warm water and soak overnight.

2 The next day, drain the beans and place them in a saucepan of cold water. Bring to the boil and simmer for 1 hour or until just tender. Drain, reserving a ladle or two of the cooking water.

3 Heat the olive oil in a medium saucepan. Add the chili flakes and garlic, and sauté briefly until the garlic is golden. Add the prosciutto and stir over moderate heat until beginning to brown (about 2 minutes). Add the lima beans and cook, tossing occasionally, until heated through (about 3 minutes) adding some of the reserved cooking water if the mixture seems a little dry.

4 Season with salt and pepper and add the torn basil leaves and arugula. Toss gently then serve warm.

Serves 4

Pork Mains

Rich and Tasty Pork Chops

Ingredients

4 large pork chops
1 tsp olive oil
1 large onion, chopped
2 cloves garlic, crushed
½ cup chopped celery
½ red bell pepper, chopped
3 small eggplant, sliced
1 jar (10 oz/300 g) salsa dip
12 black olives

Method

1 Brown the pork chops in hot olive oil in an electric frying pan lined with the baking paper. Place the chops on top of the paper.

2 Remove from the frying pan and cook all the vegetables until soft.

3 Add the chops, salsa, and olives. Simmer on a very low heat for 1 hour. Serve with creamy mashed potato and pumpkin and a fresh green vegetable.

Serves 4

Pork Loin Steaks with Fresh Herbs and Mustard

Ingredients
1½ tbsp seeded mustard
1 tbsp freshly chopped chives
1 tbsp freshly chopped cilantro
1 tbsp freshly chopped basil
2 tsp olive oil
4 lean pork loin or leg steaks

Method
1 Combine the mustard, chives, cilantro, basil, and oil in a bowl; stir well. Rub the herb mustard over both sides of the steaks.

2 Cook on lightly oiled grill over medium-high heat for 2–3 minutes on each side, depending on thickness. Allow the pork to rest for a few minutes before serving.

3 Serve with garlic mashed potato and steamed mixed beans.

Serves 4

Pork Casserole

Ingredients
1 oz/30 g butter
2 onions, chopped
1 lb/500 g lean diced pork
3 large apples, peeled, cored and chopped
1 tbsp dried mixed herbs
3 cups chicken bouillon
freshly ground black pepper

Apple Sauce
1 oz/30 g butter
2 apples, peeled, cored and chopped
2 tbsp snipped fresh chives
14 oz/400 g canned tomatoes, undrained and mashed
1 tsp cracked black peppercorns

Method
1 Heat butter in a large frying pan and cook the onions and pork over a medium heat for 5 minutes. Add the apples, herbs, bouillon, and black pepper to taste, bring to the boil, then reduce the heat and simmer for 1 hour, or until the pork is tender. Using a slotted spoon remove the pork and set aside.

2 Push the liquid and solids through a sieve and return to the pan with the pork.

3 To make the sauce, melt butter in a frying pan and cook the apple over a medium heat for 2 minutes. Stir in the chives and tomatoes and bring to the boil, reduce the heat and simmer for 5 minutes. Pour into the pan with the pork and cook over a medium heat for 5 minutes longer. Just prior to serving, sprinkle with the cracked black peppercorns.

Serves 4

Pork Loin Steaks with Fresh Herbs and Mustard

Pork Steaks and Salsa Verde

Ingredients

6 ripe tomatoes
2¼ fl oz/65 mL olive oil
salt and pepper
4–6 pork (scotch) steaks

Salsa Verde
3 cups mixed fresh herbs (basil, chives, dill, parsley)
1 tbsp capers
1 tbsp mustard
2 anchovy fillets
1 tbsp white wine vinegar
¼ olive oil

Method

1 Cut the tomatoes in half, place in ovenproof dish, drizzle with olive oil, and season with salt and pepper.

2 Roast in a 400°F/200°C/Gas Mark 6 oven for approximately 45 minutes.

3 Make the salsa by combining the herbs, capers, mustard, anchovies, and vinegar in a food processor; finely chop and add the oil. (Alternatively, very finely chop all the ingredients with a knife, then add the olive oil.)

4 Barbecue or char-grill the pork; cook for approximately 6–8 minutes.

5 Serve with the salsa and tomatoes.

Serves 4–6

Pork and Mushroom Risotto

Ingredients

2 oz/55 g butter

2 tbsp olive oil

1 onion, chopped

3 cloves garlic, crushed

1 1/2 cups arborio rice

1 cup white wine

5 cups salt reduced chicken bouillon

8 oz/225 g pork stir-fry strips

1 lb/500 g button mushrooms, sliced

1/2 cup fresh cream

1/2 cup grated Parmesan cheese, plus extra for serving

12 sprigs fresh parsley, chopped

1/4 cup chopped bell pepper

Method

1 Heat the butter and oil in a heavy-based frying pan.

2 Sauté the onions and garlic, add the rice and sauté until well coated. Add the wine and stir until absorbed

3 Add the hot bouillon in small quantities, stir well, and gently simmer until the rice is creamy. This takes about 20 minutes.

4 Stir in the pork, mushrooms, cream, Parmesan, parsley, and bell pepper.

5 Taste and adjust the seasoning accordingly. Rest for 2–3 minutes.

Note: For an extra twist, serve with lemon, toasted pine nuts, crispy prosciutto and Parmesan. Add 1 cup water to 4 cups chicken bouillon to reduce the salt.

Serves 4

Pork and Cilantro Stir-Fry

Ingredients

2 tbsp finely chopped cilantro root and stem
1 tsp freshly grated ginger
1 tsp chili paste
1 lb/500 g lean pork stir-fry strips
1 1/2 tbsp fish sauce
1 tbsp fresh lime juice
1/2 tsp brown sugar
3 tbsp vegetable oil
1 medium red onion, cut into wedges
3 oz/85 g button mushrooms, sliced
3 oz/85 g shiitake mushrooms, sliced
7 oz/200 g snow peas, trimmed and sliced
1 tbsp chopped fresh cilantro leaves
cooked noodles to serve
deep-fried lemon grass threads to serve

Method

1 Combine the cilantro root, stem ginger and chili, and rub into the pork. Stir the fish sauce, lime juice and in the brown sugar. Marinate for 10 minutes.

2 Use 2 tablespoons oil to cook the pork. Heat half the oil in a large wok over a medium-high heat, add half the pork, and stir-fry for 1–2 minutes, stirring continuously. Transfer to a plate and cover loosely with foil and set aside. Repeat with the remaining pork.

3 Reduce the heat to medium, add the remaining oil and cook the onion for 2 minutes. Add the mushrooms, pork, snow peas, cilantro leaves, and combine marinade and cook for 2–3 minutes.

4 Serve with cooked noodles and fried lemon grass.

Serves 4

Pad Thai with Pork and Shrimp

Ingredients

½ lb/250 g rice noodles

4 tbsp groundnut oil

2 cloves garlic, chopped

1 shallot, chopped

4 oz/125 g pork fillet, cut into 5 mm/¼ in thick strips

1 tbsp fish sauce

1 tsp sugar

juice of ½ lime

1 tbsp light soy sauce

1 tbsp tomato ketchup

7 oz/200 g fresh bean sprouts

4 oz/125 g cooked peeled shrimps, defrosted if frozen

black pepper

2 oz/55 g roasted salted peanuts, chopped

1 tbsp chopped fresh cilantro

1 lime, quartered, to serve

Method

1 Prepare the rice noodles according to the packet instructions. Drain and rinse. Heat a wok, then add the oil. Stir-fry the garlic, shallot, and pork for 3 minutes or until the pork turns opaque. Stir in the rice noodles and mix thoroughly.

2 Mix together the fish sauce, sugar, lime juice, soy sauce, and ketchup, then add to the noodle mixture, stirring well. Stir-fry for 5 minutes. Mix in the bean sprouts and shrimps and stir-fry for a further 5 minutes or until the bean sprouts are tender. Season with black pepper.

3 Transfer the mixture to a serving dish. Sprinkle the peanuts and cilantro over the top and serve with the lime wedges. Who can resist this mixture of sizzling pork, lime and seafood? In Thailand, you can smell the aromas from this dish wafting from the food stalls that line the streets.

Serves 4

Nasi Goreng

Ingredients

9 oz/250 g long-grain rice

1 tsp ground turmeric

3 tbsp vegetable oil

1 bunch of scallions, thinly sliced

1 in/2½ cm piece fresh root ginger, finely chopped

1–2 fresh red chilies, deseeded and thinly sliced

8 oz/225 g pork fillet, trimmed of any excess fat and thinly sliced

2 cloves garlic, crushed

3 tbsp soy sauce, or to taste

7 oz/200 g cooked peeled shrimps, defrosted if frozen and thoroughly dried

juice of ½ lemon

fresh cilantro to garnish

Method

1 Cook the rice with the turmeric, according to the packet instructions. Drain, then spread on a large plate. Leave to cool for 1 hour or until completely cold, fluffing up occasionally with a fork.

2 Heat 2 tablespoons of the oil in a wok or heavy-based frying pan. Add half the scallions, the ginger, and chilies and stir-fry over a low heat for 2–3 minutes, until softened. Add the remaining oil, increase the heat to high, then add the pork and garlic and stir-fry for 3 minutes.

3 Add the rice in 3 batches, stirring after each addition to mix well with the other ingredients. Add the soy sauce and shrimps and stir-fry for 2–3 minutes, until hot. Transfer to a bowl and mix in the lemon juice. Sprinkle with the remaining scallions and garnish with cilantro.

Serves 4

Rosemary Pork with Lentils and Apples

Ingredients

1 lb/500 g pork fillet

12 sprigs fresh rosemary

canola cooking spray

2 Granny Smith apples, peeled, cored and cut into ¾ in/2 cm thick wedges

2 tbsp red wine vinegar

1 cup reduced salt chicken or vegetable bouillon

1 tbsp canola spread, melted

¼ tsp ground cloves

1 cup red lentils

1 bay leaf

Method

1 Preheat the oven to 400°F/200°C/Gas Mark 4. Trim any excess fat or sinew from the pork fillet. Cut the pork into 12 even slices and push a sprig of rosemary through the center of each.

2 Lightly spray a non-stick frying pan with canola spray, heat over a medium high heat until hot, then cook the pork in batches for a couple of minutes until browned all over. Transfer to a baking dish.

3 Put the apples in the frying pan and cook until browned. Transfer to the baking dish. Add the vinegar and bouillon to the pan, scraping the bottom to release any juices that may be stuck to the bottom. Pour over the pork and apple. Brush the apple with the melted canola and sprinkle with the ground cloves. Bake for 10 minutes or until the pork is tender, then rest it.

4 While the pork is cooking, put the lentils and bay leaf in a small pot, just cover with water, and bring to the boil. Cook over a high heat for 15 minutes or until tender; drain and remove the bay leaf.

5 Serve the lentils topped with apples, pork, and cooking juices. Serve with steamed green vegetables.

Serves 4

Ham and Cheese Tortellini with Sage Butter

Ingredients

3 oz/85 g sweet butter

1 clove garlic, very finely chopped

20 fresh sage leaves, finely chopped, salt and black pepper

2 x 10 oz/285 g packs fresh smoked ham and cheese tortellini

2 oz/55 g Parmesan cheese, freshly grated, plus extra to serve

Method

1 Place the butter, garlic, and sage in a small heavy-based saucepan and heat over a low heat for 1–2 minutes, until the butter has melted. Season with pepper.

2 Cook the pasta in plenty of boiling salted water, until tender but still firm to the bite. Drain and transfer one-third to a warmed bowl. Toss with 1 tablespoon of the sauce and 2 tablespoons of the Parmesan. Repeat with another third of both the pasta and the sauce, then add the remaining pasta and top with the rest of the sauce and the Parmesan. Toss thoroughly, then serve with extra Parmesan.

Note: Fresh sage is the key ingredient in this dish. Without being overpowering, its flavor and aroma turn a classic cheese and ham pasta into something much more unusual.

Serves 4

147

Roasted Honey Pork Scotch

Ingredients

3–4 lb/1 1/2–2 kg pork scotch roast

salt

Marinade

1/4 cup honey

1/4 cup vegetable oil

1/4 cup orange juice

1 tbsp orange rind

Sauce

1/4 cup chicken bouillon

1 tbsp white wine vinegar

2 tbsp honey

3 tbsp Grand Marnier

2 tsp cornstarch

2 oranges, segmented

1/3 cup walnut pieces

Method

1 Combine the marinade ingredients. Marinate the pork for 1–2 hours, if desired, turning occasionally.

2 Pre-heat the oven to 425°F/220°C/Gas Mark 7. Place the pork in an oven dish, lightly sprinkle with salt and, roast for about 15 minutes, or until it starts to color. Brush with the marinade and reduce the heat to 350°F/180°C/Gas Mark 4. Cook until medium-done and the juices run light pink to clear (internal temperature 149°F/65°C). Allow about 25–30 minutes cooking time per 18 oz/510 g.

3 Allow the pork to rest for about 15 minutes in the warm oven. To make the sauce stir all the ingredients and bring to a simmer; add the oranges and walnuts at the end.

Note: Use the marinade as a baste during cooking. Smaller roasts with no rind can be quickly seared in a frying pan first, then roasted at 340°F/170°C/Gas Mark 4. Bone-in roasts should be cooked to an internal temperature of 160°F–170°F/71°F–76°C

Serves 8–16

Pork in Walnut Sauce

Ingredients

3 1/4 lb/1 1/2 kg lean pork (any joint will do)
coarse salt and freshly ground black pepper
1/2 oz/15 g butter
freshly grated nutmeg
1 tbsp brandy
4 cups milk
5 oz/145

Method

1 Sprinkle the pork with salt and leave for about 1 hour. Preheat the oven to 400°F/200°C/Gas Mark 6.

2 Rub the meat with the butter, and season it with nutmeg and pepper. Brown in a pan on all sides, then flame with the brandy. Place the meat on a low rack (or upturned plate) in a fairly deep dish that will hold the meat snugly, cover with the milk and cook in the oven for about 1 1/2 hrs. (You can also cook it on top of the stove over a low flame if you prefer.) After about 1 hour, add the walnuts. Adjust the seasoning. You can add more milk if necessary.

3 When the meat is cooked, remove it, slice it, and serve the sauce separately.

Note: Mashed potato is the best accompaniment. Baked apple slices also go well. Just slice the apples and bake them with a little butter, salt, a few drops of lemon juice, and a pinch of cinnamon.

Serves 6

Pork Mini Roast with Lemon Herbs

Ingredients

2 lb/900 g mini pork roast
3 tbsp olive oil
3 tbsp lemon juice
3 cloves garlic, crushed
2 tbsp Italian seasoning

Method

1 Mix all the ingredients together and evenly coat the pork roast. Cover and refrigerate for about 1 hour.

2 Preheat the oven to 350°F/180°C/Gas Mark 4. Calculate the cooking time; allow approximately 40 minutes per 18 oz/510 g.

3 Place the pork in a roasting pan and cook for about 80 minutes or until cooked. For a moist and tender result, avoid overcooking and cook until medium-well done. To test, gently insert a clean skewer and remove; the juices should run clear (internal temperature minimum 158°F/70°C).

4 Rest for 10 minutes in a warm oven after cooking. Carve across the grain and serve with instant seasoned vegetables.

Note: Lean pork mini roasts require brushing with pan juices during cooking. Cover and cook with a few slices of bacon if desired. Brown the roast by increasing the oven temperature towards the end of cooking.

Serves 4

Stir-Fry Pork with Water Chestnuts

Ingredients

- 2 tbsp groundnut oil
- 2 cloves garlic, crushed
- 1/2 in/1 cm piece ginger, chopped
- 1 lb/455 g pork stir-fry strips
- 1 onion, sliced
- 1 lb/455 g mixed green cabbage and bell pepper, cut into bite sized pieces
- 8 oz/225 g can water chestnuts, sliced
- 3 tbsp salt-reduced soy sauce
- 2 tbsp sake or rice wine (optional)
- 3 scallions, sliced

Method

1 Gather all your equipment and the prepared ingredients before starting cooking. Heat a wok until hot. Add a drizzle of oil, stir-fry the garlic and ginger until fragrant. Stir-fry pork in 1–2 batches. Cook the pork for about 1–2 minutes until medium-done then remove.

2 Add a little more oil, stir-fry the onions and vegetables until just done. Return the pork to the wok. Add the water chestnuts, soy sauce, and sake to taste.

3 Heat through, taste and sprinkle with the scallions. Serve with steamed rice and some chili sauce.

Serves 4

Corn and Bacon Flan

Ingredients

Pastry

1 1/2 cups all-purpose flour

pinch of salt

2 oz/55 g butter

3 tbsp cold water

Filling

4 oz/125 g lean bacon

1 small onion

1 1/2 cups corn kernels

2 large eggs

1 cup cream or milk

1/2 cup grated Parmesan cheese

pepper

Method

1 Sift the flour and salt into a bowl. Cut the butter into small pieces and rub into the flour until the mixture resembles breadcrumbs. Mix to a firm dough with the water; adding a little more if necessary. Wrap in plastic and chill for at least 30 minutes.

2 Preheat the oven to 375°F/190°C/Gas Mark 5. Roll out the dough to fit a 12 in/30 cm flan dish. Place the dough in the dish and trim the edges. Line the dough with a square of soft waxed paper and quarter-fill with dried beans or rice. Bake for 10 minutes. Remove the paper and beans and bake a further 5 minutes. (Leave the oven on)

3 Cut the bacon into small dice and fry lightly in its own fat. Scatter the bacon over the base of the pastry. Sauté the onion in the bacon fat until soft, and stir in the corn. Spoon into the pastry case.

4 Beat the eggs with the cream or milk, and half the grated cheese, adding pepper to taste. Pour over the corn and sprinkle with the rest of the cheese. Bake for 35–40 minutes. Oven temperature 375°F/190°C/Gas Mark 5.

Serves 4

Pork Fillet, Noodle, and Sugar Snap Stir-Fry

Ingredients

4 oz/125 g thick, dried rice stick noodles

1 tbsp soy bean oil

12 fl oz/350 g pork fillet, thinly sliced

4 scallions, sliced

1 red bell pepper, thinly sliced

7 oz/200 g sugar snap peas, trimmed

10 oz/285 g asparagus, cut into 1 1/2 in/4 cm pieces

1 bunch choy sum, roughly chopped

3 tbsp reduced-salt soy sauce

3 tbsp mirin (rice wine)

1 tbsp sugar

Method

1 Put the noodles in a large bowl, cover with boiling water, and allow to stand for 10 minutes, or until soft. Drain well.

2 Heat the oil in a wok until very hot, add the pork fillet slices, and stir-fry over a high heat until browned, just tender and cooked through. Remove and set aside.

3 Add the scallions and bell pepper to the wok with 2 tablespoons of water and cook until the bell pepper is soft.

4 Add the remaining vegetables to the wok and stir-fry until bright green and tender.

5 Return the pork to the wok along with the noodles. Stir in the combined soy, mirin, and sugar and cook just until the sauce thickens slightly.

Serves 4

Sausages have always been a favorite menu choice. The variety of sausages now available has lifted the humble sausage into the gourmet class. Try your local butcher for flavorsome sausages such as bratwurst, chorizo, kransky, and weisswurst, just to name a few.

Sausages

Chorizo and Lentil Stew

Ingredients

8 oz/225 g continental lentils, rinsed
4 tomatoes
8 oz/225 g piece of chorizo sausage, skinned and chopped
1 red onion, finely chopped
2 cloves garlic, crushed
½ tsp dried crushed chilies
4 cups chicken bouillon
salt and black pepper
chopped fresh Italian parsley to garnish

Method

1 Place the lentils in a large saucepan with 4 cups of water, and bring to the boil. Simmer, uncovered, for 20 minutes, stirring occasionally. Meanwhile, place the tomatoes in a bowl and cover with boiling water. Leave for 30 seconds, then peel, remove the seeds, and roughly chop the flesh. Drain the lentils and rinse under cold running water.

2 Put the chorizo into a large flameproof casserole dish and place over a low heat until the fat starts to run out. Increase the heat to high and cook, stirring frequently, for 5–8 minutes, until browned.

3 Reduce the heat to low, add the onion and fry for 4 minutes or until softened, then stir in the chopped tomatoes, garlic, and chilies. Add the lentils and bouillon, season and bring to the boil. Cover and simmer for 40 minutes, stirring occasionally, until quite thick but not too dry. Garnish with parsley.

Serves 4

Baked Conchiglie with Sausages and Mustard

Ingredients

2 tbsp olive oil

1 tbsp chopped fresh rosemary

1 tbsp chopped fresh sage

2 cloves garlic, chopped

1 lb/500 g pack best quality pork sausages, skinned and chopped

4 tbsp dry white wine

1 lb/500 g fresh pasta shells

1 oz/30 g butter

3 tbsp dried breadcrumbs

Béchamel

3 oz/85 g sweet butter

2 oz/55 g all-purpose flour

3 cups whole milk

1 1/2 oz/45 g Parmesan cheese, freshly grated

1 1/2 oz/45 g Gruyère cheese, grated

2 tsp Dijon mustard

salt and cayenne pepper

Method

1 Preheat the oven to 400°F/200°C/Gas Mark 6. Heat the oil in a frying pan, then gently fry the herbs and garlic for 1 minute. Add the sausages and fry for 10 minutes or until cooked, stirring often. Add the wine and cook for 2–3 minutes to reduce slightly.

2 To make the béchamel sauce, melt the butter over a low heat, then stir in the flour until it forms a paste. Remove from the heat and gradually add the milk, stirring. Return to the heat and cook, stirring, for 3–4 minutes, until simmering. Stir in the Parmesan, Gruyère, mustard, and a pinch of salt and cayenne.

3 Meanwhile, cook the pasta in plenty of boiling salted water, until tender but still firm to the bite. Drain and mix with the sausage mixture. Grease a 30 cm x 20 cm/12 in x 8 in ovenproof dish with half the butter, then sprinkle with half the breadcrumbs. Spoon in the pasta and sausage mixture and pour the sauce over. Sprinkle with the remaining breadcrumbs, dot with the remaining butter, then bake for 15 minutes. Preheat the broiler to high, then broil the bake for 2–3 minutes to brown the top.

Note: It's not just the British who like sausages ... this really rich, spicy Italian pasta bake is perfect as a winter treat.

Serves 4

Quick Sausage Sizzle

Ingredients

4 1/2 lb/2 kg pork or beef sausages

2 1/4 lb/1 kg onions, thinly sliced

Honey and Chili Marinade

1/2 cup olive oil

1 chili, ground

1 tbsp honey

1 tbsp crushed garlic

2 bay leaves, crushed

Method

1 Place the sausages in a large saucepan and cover with cold water. Heat slowly to simmering point, then simmer for 5 minutes. Drain well. If not required immediately, refrigerate until needed.

2 Combine all ingredients for the marinade. Heat the barbecue until hot and grease the grill bars with oil. Pour the honey and chili marinade into a heatproof bowl and place at the side of the barbecue. Arrange the sausages from left to right on the grill bars or hotplate and brush with the marinade. Turn and brush with marinade after 1 minute and continue turning and basting for 10 minutes until the sausages are well glazed and cooked through. Give a final brushing with marinade as they are removed to a serving platter.

3 Oil the hot plate and fry the onion slices. Toss at intervals and drizzle with a little oil as they cook. Serve the honey and glazed sausages with the onions and accompany with salad and garlic bread.

Note: This method is suitable for cooking a large number of sausages to serve around. Pork or beef sausages, are simmered in water before placing on the barbecue. This prevents the thick sausages from splitting and reduces the cooking time on the barbecue.

Serves 6

Italian Sausage with Zucchini and Mezuma Leaves

Ingredients

²/₃ fl oz/20 mL olive oil
**2 medium zucchinis,
    cut into ½ in/1 cm slices**
**12 oz/340 g Italian sausages
    (5–6 sausages)**
**1 thin French stick, cut into
    1 in/2 cm slices**
1⅓ fl oz/40 mL olive oil, extra
2 bunches mezuma leaves, washed
¼ cup basil leaves, shredded
4 oz/125 g semi sun-dried tomatoes
¼ cup Parmesan cheese, grated

Dressing
¼ cup olive oil
2 tbsp lemon juice
freshly ground pepper and salt

Method

1 Lightly brush a char grill frying pan with oil, and heat. Char-grill the zucchini slices for 2–3 minutes on each side, then remove and set aside.

2 Add the sausages and cook for 6–8 minutes, turning frequently, then remove from the grill and set aside to cool. Slice the sausages into 1 in/2½ cm slices.

3 Brush the slices of bread with oil, and cook on char-grill for 2–3 minutes on each side. Combine mezuma leaves, basil, sausages, zucchini, sun-dried tomatoes, and Parmesan in a large bowl.

4 Mix together the oil, lemon juice, and salt and pepper, and whisk. Drizzle the dressing over the salad.

Serves 4–6

Honey-Glazed Thick Straight Sausages

Ingredients

4 1/2 lb/2 kg thick pork or beef sausages

Honey and Chili Marinade
1/2 cup olive oil
1 chili, ground
1 tbsp honey
1 tbsp crushed garlic
2 bay leaves, crushed

Method

1 Smooth each sausage out straight and carefully push a skewer through the center end-to-end. Don't go off center or the sausage will curl. If using long metal skewers, thread 2 sausages. Combine all ingredients for the marinade.

2 Heat a barbecue to normal for indirect heat and medium for direct heat. Grease the grill bars or hotplate and arrange the sausages on the grill. Roll the sausages back and forth to gradually heat all the sides evenly until there is a color change. (This gradually expands the skin and the sausages will not burst.)

3 Continue as follows: For a kettle or hooded barbecue - place over indirect heat and brush with marinade. Cover with the lid and cook for 20–25 minutes. Brush with marinade on all sides 3 more times during cooking. Remove the skewers for final cooking. Flat-top gas or electric barbecue grills. Place a sheet of baking paper under the sausages, brush with marinade and turn frequently. Cook for 20–25 minutes until well glazed and cooked through. Remove the skewers for final cooking.

Serves 4

Chicken is a light, tender meat which makes it easy to chew and easy to digest, so it is especially suitable for infants, children and the elderly. When the skin is removed, chicken is even lower in fat, making it an ideal food for everyone.

Poultry

Poultry Appetizers, Snacks, & Salads

Lavash Rolls

Ingredients

oil spray
2 lb/1 kg chicken tenderloins
1 packet of lavash flat bread
12 oz/340 g jar mayonnaise
1 small lettuce, shredded
½ bunch of scallions, chopped
4 tomatoes, sliced
1 tub hummus
2 tbsp lemon juice
salt and pepper, to taste

Method

1 Spray a heated non-stick pan or griddle plate with oil spray and cook the tenderloins for 2 minutes on each side.

2 Place each lavash sheet on a work surface. Spread lightly with mayonnaise and sprinkle with shredded lettuce, leaving the bottom 1½ in/4 cm uncovered. Sprinkle the scallions over the lettuce and place the tomato slices on top. Place 3 or 4 tenderloins down the center and drizzle with a little hummus thinned down with lemon juice.

3 Turn up the bottom edge to hold in the filling and roll from the side into a tight roll. Wrap the bottom half in waxed paper or foil and serve.

Serves 4

Spicy Satay Skewers

Ingredients

1 lb/500 g chicken thigh fillets
salt and pepper
1 tbsp lemon juice
1 clove garlic, crushed

Satay Sauce
¾ cup peanut butter
¾ cup water
2 tbsp brown sugar
⅛ tsp chili powder, or to taste
1 tbsp soy sauce
1 tbsp grated onion
2 tbsp toasted sesame seeds

Method

1 Mix all the sauce ingredients together in a saucepan, and heat to a simmer for 5 minutes then allow to cool.

2 Cut the thigh fillets in half down the center. Cut the thinner side into 2 pieces and the thicker side into 3 pieces. Place in a bowl and sprinkle with salt, pepper, lemon juice, and garlic, and stir to mix through.

3 Pour the lemon marinade over the chicken, cover, and stand to marinate in the refrigerator for at least 1 hour or leave overnight.

4 Soak 8–10 bamboo skewers in water. Thread 4 or 5 pieces of chicken onto each skewer until almost touching. (If pushed too close together, the center of the chicken will not cook sufficiently.)

5 Heat a barbecue and oil the grill bars. Place a wire cake-rack over the grill bars. Arrange the skewers on the rack and cook on fairly high heat for 15 minutes, turning frequently, and brushing with the remaining marinade. Transfer straight onto the grill plate and cook for a further 5 minutes to brown and cook through.

6 Sprinkle with toasted sesame seeds. Serve hot with the satay sauce, boiled rice, and a spoonful of fruit chutney.

Serves 4

Easy Crumbed Chicken

Ingredients
1 lb/500 g chicken breast fillet, sliced
sprinkle of lemon pepper seasoning
1 tsp all-purpose flour
1 egg
dry breadcrumbs
2 tbsp olive oil
salt, to taste
fresh lemon
fresh chives, chopped
fresh parsley, chopped

Method
1 Slice the chicken breast into thin slices and place in a snap lock resealable bag. Sprinkle the chicken with the lemon pepper seasoning. Seal the bag and shake gently until the lemon pepper seasoning is spread evenly over the chicken.

2 Sprinkle in the flour to coat the chicken and shake in the resealable bag until it is evenly coated. Break the egg into the bag and hold the top of the bag securely as you massage the egg into the other ingredients. Finally, add the breadcrumbs and once again seal the bag and shake until the chicken is coated.

3 Line an electric frying pan with baking paper and pour in the olive oil, on top of the paper. Add the crumbed chicken and cook until it browns. Add salt to taste, turn the chicken and squeeze on some lemon. Add the fresh chopped chives and parsley, then cover and cook for approximately 3 minutes more.

Serves 4

Thai Chicken Meatballs

Ingredients

1 lb/500 g ground chicken
2 tbsp finely chopped fresh chives
2 tbsp finely chopped fresh parsley
1 level tspn Thai seasoning
1 tsp finely chopped fresh ginger
1 egg
1/2 cup fresh white breadcrumbs
salt and pepper, to taste
1 tbsp cornstarch
2 tbsp groundnut oil
1 tsp sesame oil
2 tbsp finely chopped fresh cilantro

Method

1 Combine all the ingredients except the cornstarch, the groundnut and sesame oils, and the cilantro. Form the mixture into mini meatballs.

2 Coat with the cornstarch and fry in a small amount of peanut oil with a splash of sesame oil. Cook the meatballs for approximately 3 minutes on each side, until cooked through.

3 Garnish with the cilantro and serve with chili sauce for dipping.

Serves 4

Chicken and Endive Salad with Creamy Dressing

Ingredients

- 1 slender French bread stick (baguette)
- 1 glove garlic, crushed
- 2 tbsp oil
- 1 bunch frisée, washed and drained dry
- 4 scallions, sliced
- 8 oz/250 g can mandarin segments, drained (juice reserved)
- 8 oz/250 g chicken tenderloins

Dressing
- 1 cup coleslaw dressing
- 1 tsp Dijon mustard

Method

1 Cut the bread stick into $1/5$ in/$1/2$ cm slices. Mix the garlic and oil together and brush onto bread slices. Place on a tray in a 335°F/170°C/Gas Mark 3 oven and cook until crisp and golden. Break the endive into 2 in/5 cm pieces; mix with the scallions and mandarin segments.

2 Cook the tenderloins in a lightly greased non-stick frying pan for 2 minutes on each side.

3 Mound the croûtons and endive salad onto individual serving plates and arrange the chicken on top. Mix the dressing ingredients together and pour over, allowing it to run down the sides. Serve as an entrée.

Serves 4

Chicken Vegetable Soup

Ingredients

2 skinless chicken breast fillets
4 cups reduced- salt chicken bouillon
1 tbsp canola oil
2 leeks, washed and thinly sliced
2 carrots, diced
2 sticks celery, diced
3 cloves garlic, crushed
6 cups young green leaves (watercress, arugula, sorrel, baby spinach), washed
3 tbsp fresh pesto
cracked black pepper, to taste

Method

1 Put the chicken in a pot, saucepan just enough chicken bouillon to cover and poach the chicken gently for about 10 minutes or until just cooked. Set aside to cool.

2 Heat the oil in a large saucepan, add the leeks and cook gently for about 2 minutes, until soft. Add the carrot, celery, and garlic, strain the chicken poaching bouillon through a fine sieve and add to the vegetables with the rest of the bouillon. Simmer for 10 minutes. Chop the greens finely, add to the soup, and cook for a further 10 minutes.

3 Tear the chicken breasts into fine shreds and add them to the soup. Stir in the pesto and season with plenty of cracked black pepper.

Serves 6

Chicken Satay with Crunchy Cabbage Salad

Ingredients

14 fl oz/400 g skinless chicken breast fillet

2 tsp peanut oil

Satay Sauce

2 tbsp peanut oil

2 cloves garlic, crushed

1 onion, finely chopped

1/4 cup peanut butter

9 1/2 fl oz/270 mL reduced fat coconut milk

1 1/2 tbsp sweet chili sauce

1 1/2 tbsp lemon juice

Crunchy Cabbage Salad

1/4 Chinese cabbage, finely shredded

1 carrot, finely shredded

1 red bell pepper, cut into fine strips

2 tbsp sesame seeds, toasted

Method

1 Soak 12 bamboo skewers in cold water for 20 minutes.

2 Cut the chicken into thin strips then thread onto the skewers.

3 Lightly brush the skewers with oil and put on a foil-lined tray. Broil under a high heat, turning a couple of times during cooking, until the chicken is tender.

4 To make the satay sauce, heat the oil in a small pot, add the garlic and onion, and cook over a medium heat for 5 minutes or until golden. Add the peanut butter, coconut milk, sweet chili sauce, and lemon juice, and simmer for 10 minutes or until the sauce thickens.

5 To make the cabbage salad, put the cabbage, carrot, bell pepper, and sesame seeds in a bowl and toss to combine.

6 To serve, place mounds of salad onto plates, top with the chicken skewers, and drizzle with the satay sauce.

Serves 4

Asian Chicken and Kaffir Lime Salad

Ingredients

2–3 (about 14 oz/400 g) skinless chicken breast fillets

4 kaffir lime leaves, finely shredded

1 lime, sliced

3½ oz/100 g Chinese (mung bean) vermicelli

9 oz/250 g green beans, halved

1 cup fresh cilantro leaves

1 cup fresh Thai basil leaves, shredded

4 scallions, thinly sliced

2 tbsp fried shallots

Dressing

2 tbsp fish sauce

2 tbsp lime juice

2 tbsp palm sugar, grated

Method

1 Put chicken breast fillets in a large deep frying pan, add the kaffir lime leaves and lime slices, and cover with water. Bring to the boil, reduce the heat to a very slow simmer, and poach the chicken for 15 minutes or until tender. Drain the chicken, reserving ¼ cup of the liquid. Allow the chicken to cool slightly then shred finely using your fingers.

2 While the chicken is cooking, put the vermicelli in a bowl and cover with boiling water. Allow to stand for 5–10 minutes or until tender, then drain well. Cook the beans until tender then drain.

3 Put the chicken, vermicelli, cilantro, basil leaves, green beans, scallions, and shallots into a bowl and toss to combine.

4 To make the dressing, put the reserved cooking liquid, fish sauce, lime juice, and palm sugar in a jug and whisk well. Pour over the salad and toss to combine.

Serves 4

189

Crunchy Chicken and Potato Salad

Ingredients

1 lb/500 g medium-sized potatoes
1 tsp salt
1 tbsp olive oil
1 large onion, finely chopped
1 clove garlic, crushed
7 oz/200 g ground chicken
1 tbsp lemon juice
salt and pepper, to taste
8 oz/250 g jar mayonnaise
1 small red chili, seeded and finely chopped (optional)
dill and lettuce leaves to garnish (optional)

Method

1 Wash and peel the potatoes and cut each into 4 or 6 wedges. Place in boiling water to cover, add salt, and cook for 20 minutes. Drain and cool.

2 Heat the oil in a large frying pan, add the onion and garlic and fry until onion is soft. Stir in the ground chicken and brown while stirring continuously. This will take about 15 minutes. Add the lemon juice and stir up, cooked pan juices. When the ground chicken is brown and crumbly, season with a little salt and pepper, remove from the heat, and cool.

3 Gently mix together cooled potatoes and 2–3 tablespoons of the crumbly ground chicken and the mayonnaise, tossing in the chopped chili. Pile into a salad bowl or platter and place remaining the ground chicken in a pile on the top. Garnish with dill feathers and surround with small lettuce leaves if desired. Serve as a luncheon salad or buffet item.

Serves 6

Curried Chicken Salad

Ingredients

1 large ready-cooked
   barbecued chicken

2 sticks celery, finely chopped

6 scallions, sliced

1/3 cup raisins, soaked

2 oz/55 g slivered almonds, toasted

7 oz/200 g mixed salad greens,
   washed and crisped

assorted fresh fruits for garnish

toasted shredded coconut
   for garnish

Dressing:

5 fl oz/145 mL mayonnaise

5 fl oz/145 mL low-fat plain yogurt

3 tbsps sweet mango relish

1 tbsp mild curry paste

2 tbsp lemon juice

2 tsp freshly grated lemon rind

Method

1 Remove the chicken meat from the bones and cut into bite-sized pieces. Toss with the celery, shallots, raisins, and almonds. Place all the dressing ingredients in a bowl and whisk until smooth.

2 Pour the dressing over the chicken, and toss to mix through. Cover and chill for 2 hours or more. Line a platter or individual plates with the salad greens and pile on the chicken mixture.

3 Garnish with fresh fruits of your choice. Sprinkle the top of the salad with toasted shredded coconut.

Serves 6

Crisp Curried Wings with Steamed Rice

Ingredients
2 lb/1 kg chicken wings
2 tbsp mild curry paste
1 1/2 cups basmati rice, rinsed
1/2 tsp salt
3 cups boiling water

Method

1 Rinse the chicken wings and pat dry with paper towel. Rub the curry paste onto the chicken wings with your fingers, covering all surfaces. Pin back the wing tip of each wing to form a triangle. Place the wings in single layer on a tray and stand for 30 minutes in the refrigerator, uncovered.

2 Meanwhile, place the rice in an 8-cup capacity casserole dish, and add the salt and boiling water. Cover with a lid or foil, and place on the lower shelf of a preheated 350°F/180°C/Gas Mark 4 oven. Cook for 40 minutes. Remove from the oven and stand covered for 5 minutes

3 Transfer the chicken wings to a wire rack placed over a baking tray. Place on the top shelf of the oven, above the rice. Cook for 20 minutes, turning once. When the rice has been removed, increase the oven temperature to 400°F/200°C/Gas Mark 6 and cook for a further 5 minutes to crisp the wings.

Serves 4

Crunchy Drumsticks

Ingredients

2 lb/1 kg chicken drumsticks

2 tbsp curry paste

2 cups vinegar-flavored corn chips or potato crisps

boiled rice or salad

mild relish for serving

Method

1 Rinse the drumsticks and pat dry. Using your fingers, rub the curry paste well into the skin of the drumsticks.

2 Crush the corn chips or potato crisps and press onto the drumsticks. Place on a rack over a shallow baking tray. Bake in a preheated oven 350°F/180°C/Gas Mark 4 for 35–40 minutes.

3 Serve hot with boiled rice and a portion of relish on the side. The drumsticks may also be served cold with salad.

Note: A shallow dish is recommended as it aids the crisping process.

Serves 4

Southern Fried Chicken Drumsticks

Ingredients

2 lb/1 kg chicken drumsticks
1 1/2 cups all-purpose flour
1 tsp salt and pepper
2 eggs
1/3 cup milk
1/2 cup vegetable oil

Method

1 Rinse the drumsticks and pat dry with paper towel. Smooth the skin over the drumstick if necessary. Mix the flour, salt, and pepper, and place on a paper-lined flat plate. Beat the eggs and milk well together in a deep plate.

2 Dip the drumsticks in the flour, then into the egg, turning to coat both sides. Place the drumsticks into the flour again, lift the end of the paper to toss flour over the drumstick and roll in the flour until well covered. Place in a single layer on a clean, flat tray.

3 Heat the oil in a large frying pan. Add the drumsticks and fry for a few minutes on each side, until just beginning to color. Reduce the heat, place a lid on the pan and cook slowly for 20 minutes, turning the chicken after 10 minutes.

4 Remove the lid and the increase heat; continue cooking until golden brown and crisp, turning frequently. Remove from the pan and drain on paper towels. Serve hot with vegetable accompaniments.

Serves 4

Chicken Fingers

Ingredients

2 lb/1 kg chicken tenderloins
1 clove garlic, crushed
2 tbsp lemon juice
1/2 tsp salt
1/4 tsp pepper
1 cup all-purpose flour
2 eggs, beaten with 1 tbsp water
1 1/2 cups dried breadcrumbs
1/2 cup canola oil

Dipping Sauce
1/2 sweet chili sauce
1 tsp soy sauce
1 tbsp honey

Method

1 Place the tenderloins in a large non-metallic dish. Add the garlic, lemon juice, salt, and pepper and marinate for 1 hour.

2 Remove from the marinade and coat with flour. Dip into the egg then cover with breadcrumbs, making sure to press the crumbs on firmly. Place in a single layer on a flat tray. (They may be refrigerated until ready for use.)

3 Combine the dipping sauce ingredients and set aside.

Serves 4

Golden Glazed Drumsticks

Ingredients

1 lb/500 g chicken drumsticks

½ tsp salt

1 cup hot water

1 tsp curry powder

2 tbsp honey

2 tsp French mustard

1 clove garlic, crushed

2 tbsp toasted sesame seeds

Method

1 Place the drumsticks in a saucepan, add the salt and hot water, cover and bring to the boil; turn down immediately and simmer for 10 minutes. Cool a little.

2 Mix together the curry, honey, mustard, and garlic, and heat a little to melt the honey.

3 Place the drumsticks on an oiled broiling rack, brush with glaze, and place under a hot broiler about 6 in/8 cm from the heat. Grill for 10–15 minutes, turning and brushing with glaze frequently. When cooked, place a paper cutlet frill on each drumstick. Sprinkle with toasted sesame seeds and serve with salad accompaniments.

Serves 4-6

Chicken Focaccia with Marinated Vegetables

Ingredients

1 lb/500 g chicken breast fillets (skin off)
1 clove garlic, crushed
salt and pepper
1 tbsp lemon juice
2 tsp olive oil
6 portions of focaccia bread; either individual or slab
1 tbsp olive oil
6 slices marinated roasted eggplant
3 oz/100 g marinated mushrooms
6 slices marinated roasted red bell pepper

Method

1 Trim the breast fillets, and take out the tenderloin. Place in a glass dish and the add garlic, seasonings, lemon juice, and oil. Cover and marinate for 30 minutes in the refrigerator. Heat a non-stick frying pan or greased griddle-plate. Sear the fillets for 1 minute on each side, then cook for 3 minutes on each side. Cook the tenderloins for 2 minutes on each side. When cooked, cut into diagonal slices. Keep hot.

2 Cut the focaccia slab into serving portions and split through the center. Split the individual breads, if using. Brush the cut surface with olive oil.

3 Place a slice of eggplant on each base, arrange the chicken slices on top and cover with the mushrooms and roasted the bell pepper. Replace the top slice. Place in a 325°F/160°C/Gas Mark 3 oven to heat for 10 minutes. Serve hot with marinated vegetables as a light meal.

Serves 6

Hot Chicken Balls with Salad and Fruity Sauce

Ingredients

1 quantity chicken rissoles (see below)
oil for frying
1/4 cup cider vinegar
1 tbsp powdered mustard
1 tbsp soy sauce
16 oz/455 g can pineapple pieces, drained (reserve juice)
2 tbsp cornstarch
2 bananas, sliced
1 lb/500 g mixed salad greens

Method

1 Prepare the rissoles as described in the recipe below. Form into small balls and fry in hot oil.

2 Place the vinegar, mustard, and soy sauce in a saucepan. Add the juice from the pineapple pieces and blend in the cornstarch. Stir over moderate heat until the sauce thickens slightly. Add the pineapple pieces, bananas, and chicken balls, and heat a little.

3 Pile the salad greens onto individual plates or onto a platter and spoon on the chicken balls and sauce.

Serves 6

Chicken Rissoles

Ingredients

1 lb/500 g ground chicken
1/2 tsp salt
1/2 tsp pepper
1/4 cup dried breadcrumbs
1 medium onion, finely chopped
2 tbsp parsley, finely chopped
juice of 1/2 lemon
1 egg
canola oil for frying

Method

1 Place the ground chicken in a large bowl, add the salt, pepper, breadcrumbs, chopped onion, parsley, lemon juice, and egg. Mix to combine well. Cover the bowl and rest the mixture in refrigerator for 20 minutes to absorb the juices and the blend flavors.

2 With wet hands, shape a heaped tablespoon of rissole mixture into an oval shape and flatten with the palm of your hand. Repeat with the remaining mixture.

3 Heat the oil in a large wok or frying pan. Coat each rissole in seasoned flour, shake off excess, and place in hot oil. Cook for 4 minutes on each side. Adjust the heat to fry at a steady pace.

4 Remove when cooked and drain on paper towel.

Makes 12 rissoles

Hot Chicken Balls with Salad and Fruity Sauce

Honey and Sesame Chicken

Ingredients

1 lb/500 g chicken tenderloins
¼ tsp sesame oil
¼ tsp five-spice powder
ground nut oil
2 tbsp cornstarch
3 tbsp honey
1 tbsp lemon juice
2 tbsp sesame seeds

Batter
¼ cup cornstarch
¾ cup self-raising flour
1¼ cups water
1 egg white

Method

1 Cut the tenderloins in half. Mix with the sesame oil and five-spice powder and stand for 15 minutes.

2 Meanwhile, prepare the batter by sifting the 2 flours into a bowl. Add the water and mix until free of lumps. Stiffly beat the egg white and fold into the batter.

3 Place the peanut oil in the wok or frying pan to heat. Dip a piece of chicken into the cornstarch, shake off any excess, dip into the batter, and place immediately into the hot oil. Repeat with 5 or 6 more pieces. Cook until golden brown, then remove to a tray lined with paper towels. Repeat with the remainder. Drain all the oil from the wok.

4 Add the honey and lemon juice to the wok and heat through on medium heat. Add the chicken, a few pieces at a time, and coat with honey. Remove to a serving platter and sprinkle with the sesame seeds. Serve hot.

Serves 6

Ginger Wings

Ingredients

2 lb/1 kg chicken wings

2 tbsp oil

4 tbsp grated fresh ginger root

2 cloves garlic, crushed

1 tbsp soy sauce

2 tbsp sugar

3 tbsp sherry

¼ cup toasted sesame seeds

Method

1 Fold back the wing tip of each chicken wing to form a triangle. Place the wings in a large baking dish. Mix the remaining ingredients together, except the sesame seeds, and pour over the wings.

2 Place in a preheated oven at 350°F/180°C/Gas Mark 4 and cook for 25–30 minutes, until brown and cooked through. Turn once during cooking. Remove from the oven and arrange on a platter. Sprinkle sesame seeds over and serve.

Serves 8–10

Poultry Mains

Barbecued Chicken and Mushroom Patties

Ingredients

1 lb/500 g ground chicken
1/2 cup dried breadcrumbs
1 medium onion, chopped
1/2 tsp salt
1/2 tsp pepper
2 tbsp lemon juice
2 tbsp chopped parsley
1/2 cup mushrooms, chopped
vegetable oil

Method

1 Place the ground chicken in a large bowl and add the remaining ingredients, except the oil. Mix well to combine ingredients, then knead a little with one hand to make the ground chicken fine in texture. With wet hands, shape into 4 or 5 flat patties.

2 Heat the barbecue or grill to medium-high. Oil the grill bars or rack with a little vegetable oil, and place the patties on the grill. Cook for 8 minutes on each side or until cooked through. Prick with a skewer; if the juices run clear the patties are cooked. Serve hot with vegetable accompaniments. May be served with barbecue sauce.

Serves 4

Southern Barbecued Chicken

Ingredients

4½ lb/2 kg fresh chicken, cut into pieces

Southern Barbecue Sauce

12 fl oz/350 mL can tomato puree
1 cup cider vinegar
½ cup canola oil
⅓ cup Worcestershire sauce
½ cup brown sugar
¼ cup golden syrup
2 tbsp French-style mustard
2–3 cloves garlic, minced
¼ cup lemon juice

Method

1 Prepare the Southern Barbecue Sauce in advance. Place all the ingredients into a stainless steel saucepan, and stir to combine. Bring to a simmer and continue to simmer over a low heat for 15–20 minutes, stirring regularly to prevent from catching. Stand for 1 hour to allow flavors to blend. Store in sterile jars or bottles in the refrigerator (if not used immediately).

2 Cut chicken into pieces. As a 4lb/2 kg chicken is a large bird, the breast may be cut into 3 or 4 pieces each side. Heat barbecue to moderate and oil the grill plate. Lightly sear chicken pieces on all sides over direct heat about 4 minutes each side. Lift the chicken onto a plate.

3 Place 1½ cups of the sauce into a bowl and place by the barbecue. Place a sheet of baking paper over the grill bars and prick between the runs to allow ventilation. Place the chicken onto the baking paper and brush well with the sauce.

4 Close the barbecue lid and cook for 10 minutes, then lift the lid, brush with sauce, turn the chicken, brush the underside with sauce, close lid, and cook for 10 minutes. Repeat this process every 10 minutes for a total of approximately 40–50 minutes until the chicken is rich brown in color and cooked through. If the chicken is cooking too quickly, reduce the heat by turning down the gas or raking the coals to the sides. Heat extra sauce in a small saucepan on the barbecue.

5 Serve the chicken with the hot sauce and jacket potatoes (cooked on the barbecue with the chicken). Accompany with a salad. This dish is best cooked on a charcoal or gas barbecue with a lid or hood

Serves 6–8

Lemon Barbecue-Roasted Chicken with Vegetables

Ingredients

4½ lb/2 kg chicken

2 lemons

2 cloves garlic, minced

salt and pepper

2 tsp chopped fresh oregano

2 tbsp olive oil

4 medium-sized brown potatoes, peeled and quartered

1 lb/500 g pumpkin cut into portions (skin left on)

Method

1 Wash the chicken inside and out, drain, then pat dry with paper towels. Wash the lemons, then peel off the zest with a potato peeler. Dice the zest finely and juice the lemons. Mix together half of the lemon zest, lemon juice with the garlic, salt, pepper, oregano, and oil.

2 Stand the chicken in a dish and spoon half of the lemon mixture over the chicken and in the cavity. Place the remaining zest in the cavity.

3 If using a kettle barbecue, prepare the fire for indirect heat according to manufacturer's instructions. If using a gas barbecue, preheat barbecue. Place the chicken directly onto the oiled grill over direct heat and sear on all sides. Move to indirect heat over a dripping pan.

4 Place the potatoes and pumpkin in 2 foil trays; sprinkle with the remaining lemon mixture, tossing around to coat all the pieces. Place the trays over direct heat. Cover the barbecue with lid or hood and cook for 1–1½ hours, brushing the chicken with the lemon and herb mixture every 20 minutes. Turn the vegetables.

5 Remove the vegetables when cooked and cover to keep hot. Rest the chicken for 5 minutes before carving. Serve hot with roasted vegetables and a side salad.

Serves 4

217

Chicken Puff Pie

Ingredients

2 lb/1 kg chicken thighs
2 cups water
1/2 tsp salt
1/2 tsp chicken bouillon powder
1 lb/500 g onions (4 large), chopped
2 tbsp butter
2 1/2 oz/75 g grated Romano or Parmesan cheese
1/4 tsp nutmeg
1/2 tsp freshly ground black pepper
canola oil spray
4 eggs, beaten
1 packet filo pastry

Method

1 Place the chicken thigh fillets in a saucepan and add the water and salt. Bring slowly to the boil; skim off the froth as it rises. When the water is clear, add the bouillon powder and onions. Cover and simmer for 30-35 minutes until the chicken is tender. Remove the chicken to a plate. Continue to simmer the onions, uncovered, until the onions become soft and the water has reduced.

2 Cut the chicken into strips and return to the saucepan. Add the butter and simmer for 2 minutes, stirring occasionally. Remove from the heat and allow to cool slightly. Stir to release the trapped heat. When cool, stir in the cheese, nutmeg, pepper, and beaten eggs.

3 Spray the base and sides of a metal baking dish (11 in x 10 in/28 cm x 24 cm in size) approximately with canola oil spray and line it with a sheet of filo pastry. Spray the filo with canola spray. Place a second sheet on top. Spray, then continue until all 8 sheets have been placed.

4 Pour in the chicken mixture, fold the overlapping edges over the filling. Cover the top with 8 sheets of filo, spraying with canola spray as before. Trim each the edges, allowing a slight overhang. With the tip of a sharp knife, lightly score the top 2 sheets into squares to make cutting easier once pie is cooked. Wet your hand and splash the top of the pie with water. Place in a preheated oven 350°F/180°C/Gas Mark 4 and bake for 45 minutes, until puffed and golden. Remove from the oven and rest the pie for 10 minutes before cutting through the score marks. Serve hot or cold.

Serves 8

Spicy Chicken Burritos

Ingredients

1 lb/500 g chicken stir fry strips

1 tbsp olive oil

1 large onion, finely chopped

1 clove garlic, crushed

1/2 x 13 fl oz/370 g jar tomato, onion and garlic sauce (or favorite salsa)

1/2 tsp chili powder

Toppings

1 tub guacamole

2 large onions, thinly sliced

1/2 carton sour cream

12 oz/340 g grated tasty Cheddar cheese

14 oz/400 g can refried beans, heated (optional)

12 pack Mexican tortillas

Method

1 Chop the chicken into smaller pieces. Heat the oil in a large frying pan. Add the onions and garlic, and fry until soft. Add the chicken and stir to brown on all sides. Stir in about half a jar of the tomato sauce and the chili the powder. Simmer for 15 minutes or until chicken is cooked.

2 Prepare the toppings and place in suitable serving dishes. Heat the tortillas by the method indicated on the pack. The preferred method of heating tortillas is to heat a large frying pan and heat each tortilla for 40 seconds on each side; long enough to roast slightly. Remove each tortilla, place in a clean towel, and cover. Heat the remainder and stack in the towel. Serve in the towel in a basket.

3 Invite each guest to make their own burrito by placing the chicken mixture on the tortilla then selecting their choice of toppings. Roll the buritto and enjoy.

Serves 4–6

Chicken Parmigiana

Ingredients

1 tsp olive oil
1 lb/500 g crumbed chicken schnitzel
1 jar (10 oz/285 g) salsa dip
1 cup low-fat grated cheese
sprinkle of ground paprika
fresh parsley, chopped
fresh chives, chopped

Method

1 Line an electric frying pan with baking paper and pour some olive oil on top of the paper. Cook the schnitzel on high until lightly browned. Turn and spread some of the salsa on the schnitzel until covered. Sprinkle the cheese over the schnitzel.

2 Sprinkle the schnitzels with paprika, parsley top and chives. Cover the frying pan until the cheese has melted, then serve with potato wedges and green beans.

Serves 4

Chicken, Leek, and Mushroom Flan

Ingredients

2 packets frozen savory pie flan (frozen)
1 lb/500 g chicken breast fillets (skin off)
1 tbsp canola oil
2 leeks, trimmed and thinly sliced
salt and pepper
7 oz/200 g button mushrooms, sliced
1 tbsp lemon juice
1 1/2 oz/45 g packet salt-reduced cream of chicken soup
1 cup water
1 cup milk
2 eggs, beaten
1/4 tsp nutmeg
3 oz/85 g flaked almonds

Method

1 Preheat the oven to 350°F/180°C/Gas Mark 4. Place the frozen pie flans on an oven tray and blind bake for 10–15 minutes as directed on the packet.

2 Slice the chicken breasts by placing a large knife at a 45 degree angle and slicing into 1/2 in/1 cm thick slices.

3 Heat the oil in a large pan and cook the leeks until soft. Push to the side of the pan, add the chicken, and cook for 1 minute on each side. Sprinkle lightly with salt and pepper, add the mushrooms and lemon juice, turn down the heat and simmer for 3 minutes.

4 Make the soup according to the packet directions, using 1 cup of water and 1 cup of milk. When boiling and thick, remove the soup from the heat and cool slightly. Quickly stir in the beaten egg and nutmeg.

5 Fill the 2 pie flans with the chicken, mushroom and leek, and stir any juices into the sauce. Spoon the sauce over the chicken filling, dividing equally between the two. Sprinkle each pie with half the almonds to make a dense covering. Bake for 25–30 minutes until the filling is set. Serve with a tossed salad.

Serves 8–12

Vineyard Chicken with Sautéed Mushrooms

Ingredients

2 tbsp all-purpose flour
8 basil leaves, shredded
1/4 tsp dried tarragon
1/4 tsp ground paprika
salt and freshly ground pepper
6 chicken breast halves
1 tbsp olive oil
1 tbsp butter
2 small cloves garlic, chopped
2 cups sliced mushrooms
1/2 cup dry white wine such as chardonnay or sauvignon blanc
1 cup red grapes, halved and seeded
1/2 cup real chicken bouillon
1 tsp fresh lemon juice
1 tbsp finely chopped fresh parsley

Method

1 In a wide bowl, combine the flour, basil, tarragon, paprika, salt, and pepper. Add the chicken and toss gently to coat. Heat the oil and butter in a large heavy frying pan over a moderately high heat. Add the chicken and sauté on each side until golden brown. Add the garlic and mushrooms to the pan; cook for 1 minute then pour in the wine. Cover and cook gently just until chicken is tender (about 5 minutes).

2 Add the grapes, bouillon and lemon juice, and continue cooking until the sauce is hot. Transfer the chicken and grapes to a heated serving platter and keep warm. Continue cooking the sauce until reduced by half. To serve, spoon the sauce over the chicken and garnish with the chopped parsley.

Serves 6

Tandoori Chicken

Ingredients
2 x 2 lb/1 kg fresh chickens
3 tbsp tandoori curry paste
7 oz/200 g tub plain yogurt
2 tbsp lemon juice
2 tbsp melted butter
lettuce, onion rings, tomato and lemon slices

Method

1 Rinse the chickens inside and out and pat dry with paper towels. Make deep gashes in the thighs and on each side of the breast. Pin back the wings.

2 Mix the tandoori curry paste, yogurt, lemon juice, and melted butter together. Place the chickens in a stainless steel or non-metal dish and spread the mixture all over, rubbing well into the gashes. Cover and refrigerate for 12 or more hours. Place the chickens on a roasting rack in a baking dish and spoon any remaining marinade over the chickens.

3 Place in a preheated oven 370°F/190°C/Gas Mark 5 and cook for 1 hour. Baste with the pan juices during cooking. When cooked, cover with foil and rest for 10 minutes before serving.

4 Arrange crisp lettuce leaves on a large platter and cover with onion rings. Cut the chicken into portions and place on the platter. Garnish with tomato wedges and lemon slices.

Serves 4

Oven-Baked Chicken Schnitzels

Ingredients

2 lb/1 kg chicken breast fillets (skin off)
salt and pepper
juice of 1 lemon
2 tbsp sweet chili sauce
¾ cup all-purpose flour
2 eggs
1½ cups dried breadcrumbs
olive oil spray

Method

1 Place each chicken fillet between 2 pieces of plastic wrap and flatten to an even thickness with the side of a meat mallet or a rolling pin. Place on a platter. Mix the salt, pepper, lemon juice, and chili sauce together, and pour over the chicken. Cover and refrigerate for 20 minutes.

2 Spread the flour onto a sheet of waxed paper. Beat the eggs with 1 tablespoon of water and place in a shallow tray or dish. Spread the breadcrumbs onto a sheet of waxed paper. Coat each side of the chicken fillets in flour (shake off excess), then in egg, and press into the breadcrumbs to coat both sides. Place on a flat surface in single layer. Lightly spray the schnitzels with oil spray.

3 Place the oiled side down on a rack over an oven tray (a cake-rack is suitable). Lightly spray the top-side with oil spray. Place in a preheated oven 350°F/180°C/Gas Mark 4 and cook for 8 minutes; turn with tongs and cook for 8 minutes more.

4 Serve with vegetable accompaniments or a salad.

Serves 5–6

Easy Chicken Stir-Fry

Ingredients
- 10½ oz/300 g chicken breast fillets
- 1 tbsp chili sauce with honey
- 1 tbsp hoisin sauce
- 1 tbsp soy sauce
- ½ tsp chili flakes
- 1 red bell pepper, diced
- 1 green bell pepper, diced
- 6 shallots, diced
- 1 head broccoli, separated into florets

Method
1 Slice the chicken breast fillets into thin slices. Line an electric frying pan with baking paper and heat on high. Add the chili sauce, hoisin sauce, soy sauce, and chili flakes and stir well.

2 When the sauce begins to bubble, add the chicken fillets and stir to combine. Cook for 2 minutes, add the vegetables, and stir-fry. Cover and cook for another 3 minutes, stirring regularly. Serve with boiled rice.

Serves 4

Coconut Curry

Ingredients
- 1 tbsp oil
- 4 boneless chicken breast fillets, skin removed and halved
- 2 onions, cut into eighths
- 2 cloves garlic, chopped
- 2 tbsp curry paste
- 1½ cups water
- 3 potatoes, cut into cubes
- 3 carrots, sliced
- 2 stalks fresh lemon grass, bruised, or 1 tsp finely grated lemon zest
- 1 tbsp cornstarch
- ½ cup coconut milk

Method
1 Heat the oil in a large saucepan and cook the chicken for 3–4 minutes, or until brown on both sides. Remove the chicken from the pan and set aside. Add the onions and garlic to the pan and cook over a medium heat for 4–5 minutes, or until the onions are soft. Stir in the curry paste and cook for 1 minute longer.

2 Return the chicken to the pan and stir in the water, potatoes, carrots, and lemon grass or lemon zest. Bring to the boil, then reduce the heat, cover, and simmer for 30 minutes or until chicken and vegetables are tender.

3 Whisk the cornstarch into the coconut milk. Stir the coconut milk mixture into the chicken and cook, stirring, over a medium heat for 4–5 minutes or until the curry boils and thickens. Cook for 3 minutes longer. Just prior to serving, remove the lemon grass.

Serves 4

Easy Chicken Stir-Fry

233

Quick Chicken Lasagne

Ingredients

1 lb/500 g chicken thigh fillets
salt and pepper
12½ oz/375 g jar tomato and pesto sauce
8 oz/250 g packet instant lasagne sheets
3 oz/100 g mushrooms, sliced

Topping
8 oz/250 g ricotta cheese
7 oz/200 g plain yogurt
**2 tbsp grated Romano
   or Parmesan cheese**
pinch of nutmeg
2 eggs, lightly beaten

Method

1 Place thigh the fillets between 2 pieces of plastic wrap and pound out with a meat mallet until thin. Season with salt and pepper.

2 Grease a baking dish or lasagne dish with oil. Spread a thin layer of the tomato and pesto sauce in the base of the dish. Dip 3 or 4 lasagne sheets into a dish of water, remove, and place to cover the base of the baking dish. Spread generously with the tomato sauce. Place the thigh fillets over the tomato sauce in a single layer, and cover with the sliced mushrooms. Wet 4 more lasagne sheets and layer over the mushrooms. Spread the remaining sauce over the lasagne sheets.

3 Mix all the topping ingredients together, and spread over the lasagne. Grate a little extra Parmesan over the surface and dot with small flecks of butter. Place in preheated oven at 350°F/180°C/Gas Mark 4 for 35–40 minutes.

4 Stand for 10 minutes before serving to allow the lasagne sheets to re-absorb loose moisture.

Serves 6

Creamy Mustard Chicken

Ingredients

1 tsp olive oil

1 tsp butter

1 lb/500 g lean chicken breast fillets

sprinkle of lemon pepper seasoning

2 tbsp all-purpose flour

1 tsp wholegrain or German mustard

2 tbsp cream

fresh parsley, chopped

Method

1 Heat the butter and olive oil on medium heat in a frying pan. Coat the chicken in lemon pepper seasoning and place flour in the pan. (You can cook the chicken in strips or as whole breast fillets.)

2 Add the mustard, cream, and parsley to create a delicious sauce and stir frequently. (Extra light cream can be used in this recipe, if you want lots of sauce.) Serve with mashed potato, and carrot and zucchini sticks. As an alternative to chicken, use veal, beef or pork strips.

Serves 4

Feta Drumsticks

Ingredients

1 oz/30 g butter

1 clove garlic, crushed

1 bunch English spinach, finely shredded

2 slices ham, finely chopped

4 oz/125 g feta cheese, broken into small pieces

1 tsp ground cilantro

3 tsp ground nutmeg

freshly ground black pepper

12 chicken drumsticks

2 tbsp olive oil

Method

1 Melt the butter in a frying pan and cook the garlic over a medium heat for 1 minute. Stir in half the spinach and cook for 3–4 minutes, or until the spinach is wilted. Remove the cooked spinach from the pan and set aside. Cook the remaining spinach in the same way.

2 Preheat the oven to 350°F/180°C/Gas Mark 4. Place the spinach, ham, feta cheese, cilantro, 1 teaspoon of nutmeg, and black pepper to taste in a bowl and mix to combine. Ease the skin carefully away from each drumstick to form a pocket. Place a spoonful of spinach mixture in each pocket and pull the skin over. Brush the drumsticks with oil, sprinkle with the remaining nutmeg and place in a baking dish. Bake for 30 minutes or until the drumsticks are cooked through.

Serves 6

Creamy Mustard Chicken

237

Lovely Legs and Vegetable Casserole

Ingredients

12½ oz/375 g jar tomato and pesto sauce

½ cup water

2 lb/1 kg chicken drumsticks

4 medium potatoes, peeled and quartered

2 tbsp olive oil

2 tbsp finely chopped parsley

8 oz/225 g packet frozen peas

14 oz/400 g can baby corn

Method

1 Pour the tomato and pesto sauce into a casserole or baking dish and stir in the water. Place the lovely legs in one layer and arrange potato quarters in between. Drizzle the olive oil over and sprinkle with parsley. Cover the dish with lid or foil.

2 Place in a preheated oven at 180°C/350°F/Gas Mark 4 and cook for 30 minutes. Lift from the oven and turn the legs and potatoes. Add the peas and baby corn. Return to the oven and cook, uncovered, for 25 minutes more or until the legs and potatoes are tender.

3 Serve hot with crusty bread.

Serves 4–6

Easy Apricot and Mango Chicken Loaf

Ingredients

25 oz/700 g ground chicken
1 cup fresh breadcrumbs
¾ cup scallions, chopped (including green part)
1 tbsp finely chopped parsley
2 tbsp dried apricots, dried
1 tbsp mango relish
1 egg
1 tsp salt
¼ tsp pepper
oil for greasing

Method

1 Place the ground chicken in a large bowl. Add all the remaining ingredients, except the oil. With your hand mix and knead the mixture for 2–3 minutes to combine the ingredients well and to give a fine texture.

2 Grease a 9 in x 3 in/22 cm x 8 cm x 5 cm loaf tin with oil. Pour in the ground chicken mixture. Place in a preheated oven 350°F/180°C/Gas Mark 4 for 50–55 minutes. To test the chicken insert a skewer into the center; if clear juice appears it is cooked. If the juice is a pink color, further cooking is required. Rest in the tin for 10 minutes before serving.

3 Serve hot with vegetable accompaniments or cold with salad.

Serves 6

Tangy Tenderloins

Ingredients

1 lb/500 g chicken tenderloins
salt and pepper, to taste
olive oil spray
7 oz/200 g sugar peas
14 oz baby corn, drained
$\frac{1}{2}$ cup apricot nectar
2 tbsp cider vinegar
2 tbsp sweet chili sauce

Method

1 Flatten the tenderloins slightly and sprinkle with salt and pepper. Heat a heavy-based frying pan and spray lightly with oil spray. Add the tenderloins and cook for 2 minutes on each side. Remove from the pan.

2 Add the sugar peas and stir around the pan until they brighten in color. Add the drained corn.

3 Return the chicken to the pan and toss with the vegetables. Combine the apricot nectar, vinegar, and chili sauce. Pour over the chicken and vegetables and heat through. Pile onto serving plates and serve immediately.

Serves 5

Crisp Chicken

Ingredients

1 lb/500 g chicken, strips

all-purpose flour to lightly coat

1 egg, beaten

2 tbsp olive oil

Method

1 Coat the strips of chicken in the flour and then in the egg.

2 Cook the chicken in the olive oil in an electric frying pan lined with baking paper until the chicken is golden brown. This will take approximately 3–5 minutes.

3 Serve with a crisp green salad, roasted tomatoes and hot broken bread rolls.

Serves 4

Herb Chutney Chicken

Ingredients

3 lb/1 1/2 kg chicken

2 oz/55 g butter, melted

2 cloves garlic, crushed

Chutney Stuffing

2 tbsp chopped fresh mixed herbs such as parsley, chives, rosemary, thyme and oregano

4 oz/125 g grated fresh Parmesan cheese

2 tbsp fruit relish

1 egg, lightly beaten

1 cup dried bread crumbs

3 oz/85 g butter, melted

Method

1 To make the stuffing, place the herbs, cheese, chutney, egg, breadcrumbs, and butter in a bowl and mix to combine. Fill the cavity of the chicken with stuffing and secure the opening with metal or bamboo skewers.

2 Tuck the wings under the body of the chicken and tie the legs together. Place the bird, breast side up, in a baking dish. Combine the butter and garlic, brush over the chicken and bake in a preheated 350°F/180°C/Gas Mark 4 oven, turning several times, for 1–1 1/2 hours or until the bird is cooked.

Serves 4

Crisp Chicken

Chicken Maryland

Ingredients

1 lb/500 g thinly sliced chicken breast fillets
sprinkle lemon pepper seasoning
all-purpose flour
1–2 eggs
dry breadcrumbs
1 tbsp olive oil
4 slices low-fat ham
pineapple slices
low-fat grated cheese
sprinkle ground paprika
sprinkle chives, chopped

Method

1 Coat the thinly sliced chicken breast fillets with the lemon pepper seasoning, flour, egg, and breadcrumbs.

2 Cook in the olive oil in lining an electric frying pan lined with baking paper, until golden. Top with the ham, pineapple, cheese, ground paprika, and chopped chives.

3 Cover the frying pan and allow the topping to melt. Serve with a crisp green salad and tomato wedges.

Serves 4

Chicken Steaks with Herb Sauce

Ingredients

1 lb/500 g chicken thigh fillets
1–2 tbsp butter
1 clove garlic, finely chopped
1 medium onion, finely chopped
salt and pepper
¼ cup lemon juice
1 tbsp parsley, chopped

Method

1 Pound the thigh fillets on both sides with a meat mallet to flatten.

2 Heat enough butter to coat the base of a large heavy-based frying pan. Place the thigh fillets in and cook for 3 minutes on each side over medium heat. Remove to a heated plate.

3 Add the garlic and onion, and fry over a gentle heat until the onions are soft. Add the salt, pepper, lemon juice and parsley. Stir quickly to lift the pan juices and pour over the chicken steaks. Serve immediately with vegetable accompaniments.

Serves 4

Orange-and-Spice Leg Steaks

Ingredients
6 chicken drumsticks
1 tsp ground ginger
1/2 tsp ground nutmeg
1/2 tsp ground cinnamon
2 tbsp canola oil
2 large oranges
1 tsp brown sugar

Method

1 Remove the bone and skin from each drumstick. With a sharp knife, make 3 diagonal slashes on both sides to cut through the smooth membrane covering. Place the chicken meat between 2 sheets of plastic wrap and pound each side with a meat mallet to thin out. It may be necessary to snip through more membrane as you pound.

2 Mix the ginger, nutmeg, and cinnamon together. Rub the spices all over the chicken, into the slashes, and in the center where the bone was removed. Stand for 30 minutes or more for the flavor to penetrate.

3 Heat the oil, in a large non-stick frying pan until hot. Add the chicken and sear quickly for 1 minute on each side. Turn down heat to medium and fry the chicken for 4 minutes on each side. Remove to a plate. Pour off most of the oil from the pan. Thinly peel, the zest off 1 orange with a potato peeler and cut into julienne strips or remove the zest with a zester. Juice the oranges.

4 Stir the orange juice into the pan, place over low heat, and scrape up and dissolve any cooked-on brown juices. Stir in the brown sugar and zest. Bring to a steady simmer while stirring.

5 Return the chicken to the pan, and quickly turn to coat and glaze with sauce as it thickens, taking care not to evaporate the sauce too much.

6 Transfer the chicken to serving plates and spoon the sauce over. Pile the zest on top. Garnish with orange slices and a sprigs of watercress. Serve with rice or mashed potato.

Serves 3–4

Poached Chicken with Tomato and Mushroom Sauce

Ingredients

1 medium-sized onion, finely chopped
1 clove garlic, finely chopped
3 large ripe tomatoes, blanched, peeled and chopped or 1 can peeled whole tomatoes
3 oz/100 g mushrooms, sliced
1 tbsp chopped fresh basil
¾ cup water
1 tsp dried oregano
freshly ground black pepper
2 chicken breast fillets (skin off)
1 cup pasta twists
½ tsp olive oil
grated Parmesan cheese to serve (optional)

Method

1 Place the onion, garlic, tomatoes, and mushrooms in a wide-based saucepan over moderate heat. Stir until the onions begin to soften. Add the onions, basil, water, oregano and pepper; heat a little and add the chicken breasts. Cover and simmer slowly for 20 minutes, or until the chicken is tender. Do not allow to boil.

2 In another saucepan, cook the pasta twists according to the packet instructions. Drain and stir the olive oil through.

3 When the chicken is cooked, remove it to a plate. If the sauce is too thin, turn up heat and boil until it reduces and thickens. Pour over the chicken and serve with the pasta twists. Sprinkle with Parmesan cheese.

Serves 2–3

Australian-Style Chicken Curry

Ingredients

1 lb/500 g chicken thigh fillets
2 tbsp olive oil
1 large onion, finely chopped
9 oz/280 g can Madras curry cooking sauce
2 tbsp golden raisins
2 bananas, sliced
1 green apple, peeled, cored and cut in large dice

Method

1 Cut the chicken thighs in half or into 3 pieces. Heat half the oil in a large saucepan, add one-third of the chicken and quickly brown on both sides. Remove to a plate and brown the remaining chicken in 2 batches, adding remaining oil when necessary. Remove last batch of chicken.

2 Add the onion and cook a little then stir in the Madras curry cooking sauce. Add a little water (about a $1/4$ can) to the can to rinse down remaining sauce and pour into the saucepan.

3 Bring to the boil, turn down the heat and return the chicken to the saucepan. Cover and simmer for 20 minutes. Add the golden raisins, banana and apple and simmer for 15–20 minutes more. Serve immediately with boiled rice.

Serves 4

Chicken Rolls with an Indonesian Flavor

Ingredients

2 lb/1 kg chicken thigh fillets
9½ oz/285 g can redang curry sauce
2 bananas
2 tbsp vegetable oil
½ cup water
½ cup coconut milk
1 small, fresh pineapple, peeled and thinly sliced
1–2 tbsp butter
freshly ground black pepper
2 tbsp shredded coconut, toasted
steamed rice to serve

Method

1 Open out the thigh fillets on a large chopping board. Flatten with a meat mallet to an even thinness. Spread each with a teaspoon of rendang curry sauce.

2 Peel the bananas and slit in half lengthwise, then cut in half to make 4 pieces. Place a piece of banana in the center of each fillet and form into a roll. Fasten with a toothpick. Heat the oil in a wide-based saucepan and brown the rolls on all sides, a few at a time, removing the rolls to a plate as they brown. Drain all the oil from the saucepan.

3 To the same saucepan, add the rendang curry sauce and the water. Bring to the boil, turn down heat to a simmer, add the chicken rolls. Cover and simmer for 35 minutes, turning rolls once during cooking.

4 Remove the rolls to a heated platter and keep hot. If the sauce is thin, increase the heat and reduce the sauce to a thicker consistency. Reduce the heat and stir in the coconut milk and simmer for 2 minutes. Return the rolls to the saucepan to reheat.

5 Sauté the pineapple rings in a little butter until lightly colored, and grind over some black pepper. Arrange 1 or 2 slices of pineapple and a chicken roll on each plate, spoon the sauce over the roll, and sprinkle with a little toasted coconut. Accompany with steamed rice.

Serves 4

Hawaiian Poached Chicken

Ingredients

3 lb/1 1/2 kg fresh chicken
1/2 tsp each salt and pepper
1 tsp paprika
2 tbsp oil
1 large onion, chopped
1 clove garlic, crushed
1/4 cup water
1 tbsp Worcestershire sauce
2 tsps sweet chili sauce
1/4 cup apple cider vinegar
1 1/2 tbsp brown sugar
1/2 medium fresh pineapple, peeled and diced
1 green bell pepper, seeded and cut into thin strips
1 red bell pepper, seeded and cut into thin strips
1 tbsp rum (optional)
1 1/2 tbsp cornstarch

Method

1 Joint the chicken into serving pieces. Season with salt, pepper, and paprika. Heat the oil in a large saucepan. Add the chicken pieces, a few at a time, and brown on all sides. Remove to a plate lined with paper towel as they brown.

2 Add the onion and garlic to the saucepan and cook, stirring, for 2 minutes. Return the chicken to the saucepan. Combine the water, the two sauces, vinegar, and brown sugar, and pour over the chicken. Add the pineapple pieces and bell peppers. Simmer for 25–30 minutes until chicken is tender.

3 Warm and flame the rum, if using, and pour to the chicken. Blend the cornstarch and a little water together, add to the chicken and stir through. Allow to simmer until the sauce thickens. Increase the heat until it boils then turn off immediately. Serve with boiled rice.

Serves 6

Drumsticks in Tomato Sauce

Ingredients
2 lb/1 kg chicken drumsticks
1 tbsp canola oil
1/2 x 24 oz/750 g jar capsicum, mushroom and spices sauce (or your favorite salsa)
1/2 cup water
1 cinnamon stick
1 large onion, sliced into rings
2 tbsp finely chopped parsley
8 oz/250 g spaghetti, boiled and drained
grated Parmesan cheese for serving

Method

1 Rinse the drumsticks and pat dry with paper towel. Heat the oil in a wide-based saucepan and lightly brown the drumsticks, 3 at a time. Remove from pan as they brown and finally wipe the fat from the pan with paper towel.

2 Pour in the spicy sauce, add the water, and then add the cinnamon stick. Heat the sauce then return the drumsticks to the pan. Place the onion rings in the pan and sprinkle in the parsley. Cover and bring to the boil, turn down to a simmer, and cook for 35 minutes until chicken is tender.

3 Boil and drain the spaghetti and stir through a teaspoon of oil to keep the strands separate.

4 Place in a large serving dish, arrange the drumsticks around the spaghetti, and smother with the sauce. Sprinkle with extra parsley. Serve immediately with Parmesan cheese. Accompany with a tossed side salad.

Serves 5

Chicken Wings Moroccan Style

Ingredients

2 tbsp canola oil
2 lb/1 kg chicken wings
1 large onion, finely chopped
1 clove garlic, crushed
1 1/2 tsp chopped fresh ginger
1/2 tsp ground turmeric
1/2 tsp cumin
1/2 cinnamon stick
1/4 cup cider vinegar
15 oz/425 mL can apricot nectar
salt and pepper
3 oz/85 g dried prunes, pitted
3 oz/85 g dried apricots
1 tbsp honey
1/4 cup lemon juice
steamed couscous or rice to serve

Method

1 Heat the oil in a wide-based saucepan or lidded skillet. Add the chicken wings, a few at a time, and brown lightly on both sides. Remove to a plate as they brown.

2 Add the onions and fry for 2 minutes. Stir in the garlic, ginger, and spices, and cook, while stirring, for 1 minute. Return the chicken to the pan, stir, and turn the wings to coat with spices. Add the vinegar and apricot nectar, and season to taste. Cover and simmer for 25 minutes.

3 Add the prunes, apricots, honey, and lemon juice. Cover and simmer for 10 minutes and then remove the lid and simmer, uncovered, for 5 minutes. If a thicker sauce is desired, remove the wings and fruit to a serving platter, increase the heat, and boil until the sauce reduces and thickens, stirring occasionally. Pour the sauce over the wings. Serve immediately with steamed couscous or rice.

Serves 3–4

263

Curried Chicken

Ingredients

- 1 large onion, chopped
- 1 carrot, chopped
- 1/2 cup chopped celery
- 1 tsp butter
- mild curry powder, to taste
- 8 chicken drumsticks, skin removed
- 1–1 1/2 cups hot water
- salt and pepper, to taste
- 1/2 – 3/4 cup low-fat milk
- fresh chopped parsley
- 2 tbsp all-purpose flour, mixed to a smooth paste with a little low-fat milk

Method

1 In an electric frying pan lined with bake paper, soften the vegetables in the butter, then add the curry powder to taste and cook for 30 seconds. Add the chicken, water, and salt and pepper to taste, and simmer on a low heat for 40 minutes or until the chicken is tender.

2 Drain off some of the liquid and replace it with the milk. Bring back to a simmer, add the parsley, and thicken with the flour mixture, adding it slowly and stirring until the sauce is the desired consistency. Serve with boiled rice.

Serves 4

Creamy Chicken Pasta

Ingredients

1 tbsp butter
1 lb/500 g chicken breast fillets, thinly sliced
1 clove garlic, crushed
generous sprinkle chopped chives
salt, to taste
2 tbsp fresh parsley, finely chopped
10½ fl oz/300 mL cream
sprinkle of seasoned pepper
½ lb/250 g dried pasta

Method

1   Heat half the butter on medium heat in a electric frying pan lined with paper. Add the chicken breast fillets, garlic, chopped chives, baking and a little salt.

2   Cover and cook for 4 minutes, stirring occasionally. Add the remaining butter, parsley, cream, seasoned pepper and finally the hot cooked pasta. Stir through to combine. Serve in warmed bowls

Serves 4

Hokkien Noodles with Lemon Grass Chicken

Ingredients

2 chicken breast fillets (about 14oz/400 g)
1 stalk lemon grass, halved and bruised
14 oz/400 g hokkien noodles
2 scallions, sliced
1 red bell pepper, thinly sliced
1 carrot, thinly sliced
3^1/$_2$ oz/100 g snow peas, halved
2 oz/55 g peanuts, toasted
2 tbsp sesame seeds, toasted
2 tbsp fresh Thai basil or mint leaves

Dressing
2 tbsp sweet chili sauce
1 tbsp sweet soy sauce
2 tbsp lime juice
1 tsp peanut oil

Method

1 Put the chicken breast fillets in a large deep frying pan with the lemon grass, just cover with water, and bring to a simmer. Gently poach for 10–15 minutes or until tender. Allow to stand for 5 minutes then remove from the water and shred finely. Finely chop the lemon grass and set aside to use in the dressing.

2 Gently separate the hokkien noodles and put in a large bowl. Cover with boiling water and allow to stand for 2 minutes then drain well.

3 Put the noodles, chicken, scallions, bell pepper, carrot, snow peas, peanuts, sesame seeds, and basil leaves in a large bowl and prepare the dressing.

4 To make the dressing, put the chopped lemon grass, sweet chili sauce, kecap manis, lime juice, and peanut oil in a bowl and whisk to combine.

5 Pour the dressing over the other ingredients and toss gently

Serves 4

Chicken and Vegetable Stir-Fry

Ingredients
- 2 tbsp canola oil
- 1 clove garlic, crushed
- 1 tsp finely chopped fresh ginger
- 6 scallions, sliced into 1/2 in/1 cm lengths on the diagonal
- 1 lb/500 g chicken stir-fry strips
- 2 tbsp oyster sauce
- 1/2 tsp chicken bouillon powder
- 1/4 cup water
- 7 oz/200 g snow peas, trimmed
- 1 red bell pepper, seeded and cut into strips
- 16 oz/485 g can mixed vegetables, drained

Method

1 Heat the oil in a wok, add the garlic, ginger, and scallions, stir-fry for 1 minute, then add the chicken and stirfry until cooked through. Remove the chicken and scallions from the wok.

2 Mix together the oyster sauce, bouillon powder, and water and add to the wok. Add the snow peas and bell pepper and cook, lifting the vegetables from the bottom and turning over continuously, for 2 minutes. Add the drained vegetables and continue stirring for 1 minute.

3 Return the chicken and scallions to the pan and toss the vegetables for 2 minutes. Pile onto a platter and serve immediately.

Serves 4–5

Stir-Fry Chicken with Almonds and Broccoli

Ingredients

1 lb/500 g chicken stir-fry strips
5 tsp cornstarch
1/2 tsp five-spice powder
1/2 tsp salt
oil for frying
5 oz/145 g blanched almonds
1 1/2 tsp finely chopped fresh ginger
1 clove garlic, crushed
2 tbsp dry sherry
1 tsp sugar
1 tbsp soy sauce
2 tsp water
7 oz/200 g broccoli florets, blanched
boiled rice to serve

Method

1 Place the chicken in a bowl and sprinkle over 3 teaspoons cornstarch, five-spice powder and salt. Mix well and set aside. Heat about 1 in/2 1/2 cm deep oil in the wok and fry the almonds until golden. Remove and drain; set aside. Add the ginger and garlic and stir-fry for 1 minute. Add the chicken in batches and stir-fry until the chicken turns white.

2 Return all the chicken to the wok and add the sherry, sugar, and soy sauce. Stir a little then add the combined water and remaining cornstarch. Stir, tossing, until the sauce thickens.

3 Add the broccoli and fried almonds and toss to heat through. Serve immediately with boiled rice.

Note: To blanch the broccoli, place in a saucepan of boiling water for 30 seconds or until it turns bright green. Remove immediately and plunge into a bowl of iced water. When cold, drain in a colander.

Serves 4

Chicken Supreme

Ingredients

4 small chicken breast fillet
tasty cheese, sliced
bunch fresh asparagus or 1 can
  (12 oz/340 g) of asparagus spears
sprinkle seasoned pepper
a little all-purpose flour
1 egg mixed with 1 tbsp milk
breadcrumbs to coat
a little olive oil

Method

1 Slice each chicken breast fillet in half to form a pocket. Fill with cheese, asparagus, and a sprinkle of seasoned pepper. Close each breast with toothpicks and coat with the flour, egg mixture, and breadcrumbs.

2 In an electric frying pan lined with baking paper, add the olive oil, and cook the chicken breasts on top of the paper, until golden brown. Turn and repeat. Approximately 4–5 minutes on each side, is enough.

3 Serve garnished with watercress and green beans.

Serves 4

Poussins Provencals

Ingredients

4 cloves garlic, halved lengthways

6 fresh rosemary sprigs, 4 left whole and 2 chopped, plus extra to garnish

4 oven-ready poussins (small chickens)

4 tbsp olive oil

salt and black pepper

2 tsp all-purpose flour

1¼ cups chicken bouillon or white wine

juice of ½ lemon

1 tsp Dijon mustard

Method

1 Preheat the oven to 400°F/200°C/Gas Mark 6. Place 2 pieces of garlic and 1 rosemary sprig in the cavity of each poussin, then place them on a rack in a roasting tin.

2 Brush each bird with 1 tablespoon of oil and sprinkle over the chopped rosemary. Season and roast for 50 minutes or until cooked through and tender. Remove from the oven, then loosely cover with foil to keep warm.

3 Remove the rack and pour the cooking juices into a small saucepan. Stir in the flour, then stir over moderate heat for 1–2 minutes, until smooth. Pour in the bouillon or wine and bring to the boil, stirring. Add the lemon juice and simmer for 2–3 minutes, stirring, until thickened. Add the mustard, then season. Garnish with rosemary and serve with the gravy.

Note: These tender baby chickens are infused with the flavors of garlic and rosemary. Serve with the lemony gravy, potatoes, and some sautéed zucchinis.

Serves 4

Chicken and Pear Curry

Ingredients

5 pears

1 tbsp butter

1 tbsp oil

1 lb/500 g chicken tenderloin or stir-fry strips

1 medium onion, finely chopped

1 tbsp Madras-style curry powder

1 tsp sugar

$1/2$ cup cream

$1/2$ cup white wine

2 tbsp shredded coconut

2 tbsp toasted cashew nuts

Method

1 Cut the pears into $1/2$ in/1 cm strips and set aside. Heat the butter and oil in a large frying pan, add the chicken, and brown on both sides to seal. Remove from the pan.

2 Add the onion and fry gently until soft. Stir in the curry powder and cook for 1 minute. Reduce the heat, add sugar, cream, wine, and coconut, and stir well.

3 Return the chicken to the pan and add the pears. Cover and simmer for 15 minutes, taking care not to boil. Remove to a heated dish and sprinkle with toasted cashew nuts. Serve with the boiled rice.

Serves 4

Sweet and Sour Chicken

Ingredients

14 oz/400 g can pineapple pieces
1 red bell pepper, seeded
6 scallions
2 tsp soy sauce
2 tbsp malt vinegar
2 tbsp brown sugar
1 tbsp lemon juice
1 tsp finely grated fresh ginger
2 tbsp tomato ketchap
2 tbsp water
1 tbsp cornstarch
1 lb/500 g chicken thigh fillets
3 tbsp olive oil

Method

1 Drain the pineapple pieces and reserve the juice. Cut bell pepper into strips or squares. Cut the scallions, including most of the green shoot, into $\frac{1}{2}$ in/1 cm diagonal pieces. Mix together the pineapple juice, soy sauce, vinegar, sugar, lemon juice, ginger, and tomato ketchup. Blend the water and cornstarch and set aside. Cut each thigh fillet into $\frac{1}{2}$ in/1 cm-wide strips.

2 Heat a wok, add 2 tablespoons of oil, and when hot, add one third of the chicken. Stir-fry over high heat until cooked (about 1 minute). Remove and cook the remaining chicken in 2 batches, adding extra oil if needed. Drain the chicken well on paper towels. Drain the all oil from the wok.

3 Pour the sauce mixture into the wok and add the blended cornstarch. Cook, stirring, until mixture boils and thickens. Stir in bell pepper, scallions and pineapple pieces; cook for 1 minute. Add chicken and heat through. Serve immediately with boiled rice.

Serves 6

281

Light Chicken Curry with Jasmine Rice

Ingredients

14 fl oz/400 mL reduced-fat coconut milk

1 cup salt-reduced chicken bouillon

2–3 tbsp green curry paste

3 kaffir lime leaves, finely shredded

10 oz/300 g pumpkin, peeled and chopped

4 (about 1 lb/500 g) skinless chicken breast fillets, cut into small cubes

1/2 lb/230 g can bamboo shoots, drained

10 oz/285 g snake beans, chopped

10 oz/285 g broccoli, cut into florets

1 tbsp fish sauce

1 tbsp palm sugar, grated

2 tbsp Thai basil leaves, torn

1 1/2 cups jasmine rice

2 stalks lemon grass, halved

Method

1 Put the coconut milk, bouillon, green curry paste and kaffir lime leaves in wok or large saucepan and bring to the boil. Cook over a high heat, until the sauce starts to thicken slightly. Add the pumpkin and simmer for 10 minutes or until it starts to soften

2 Add the chicken breast and bamboo shoots, reduce the heat, and simmer for 10 minutes or until the chicken is tender. Add the snake beans, broccoli, fish sauce, and palm sugar, and cook, uncovered, until the vegetables are soft.

3 Remove from the heat and stir through half the basil leaves.

4 Put the rice, lemon grass, saucepan and 4 cups of water in a saucepan, bring to the boil, and cook over a high heat until steam holes appear in the top of the rice. Reduce the heat to low, cover, and cook over a low heat for 10 minutes or until all the liquid is absorbed and the rice is tender. Transfer the rice to bowls, spoon curry and scatter with the remaining basil leaves.

Serves 4

Chicken with Ricotta, Arugula Roast, and Pepper

Ingredients

7 oz/200 g fresh ricotta
1 cup arugula, roughly chopped
¼ cup pinenuts, toasted
½ red bell pepper, roasted and finely chopped
freshly ground pepper and salt
4 small chicken breasts, with skin on
1 tbsp butter
1 cup chicken bouillon

Method

1 Preheat the oven to 400°F/200°C/Gas Mark 6.

2 Combine the ricotta, arugula, pinenuts, bell pepper, and pepper and salt in a small bowl, and mix together, until smooth.

3 Place 1–2 tablespoons of the ricotta mixture under the skin of each chicken breast. Lightly grease a baking dish. Place the chicken breasts in the dish, and sprinkle with pepper and salt. Place 1 teaspoon of butter on each breast, pour bouillon around the chicken, and bake, for 20–25 minutes.

4 Serve the chicken with the pan juices and the arugula salad.

Serves 4

Chicken with Oregano and Lemon

Ingredients
4 chicken breasts
2 tsp dried oregano
freshly ground pepper and salt
2 tbsp olive oil
1 1/4 lb/600 g potatoes, thinly sliced
1 bunch scallions, trimmed and halved
1/4 cup chicken bouillon
2 1/2 fl oz/75 mL lemon juice
2 sprigs oregano, chopped

Method
1 Season the chicken with the dried oregano, pepper, and salt.

2 Heat the oil in a large frying pan.

3 Add the chicken, potatoes, and scallions, and brown quickly for 2–3 minutes.

4 Pour in the bouillon, cover, and simmer for 10–15 minutes or until the chicken is cooked.

5 Add the lemon juice and fresh oregano. Cook for a further 3 minutes. Serve immediately.

Serves 6

Chicken with Mustard

Ingredients

8 chicken drumsticks
2 tbsp wholegrain mustard
6 oz/185 g dry breadcrumbs
1 tsp salt
1 tsp pepper
3 oz/85 g butter
3 oz/85 g all-purpose flour
2 eggs, beaten

For the Lime and Mustard Butter
5 oz/145 g butter
1 tbsp Dijon mustard
squeeze of lime juice
1/4 tsp cayenne pepper

Method

1 Make the Lime and Mustard Butter a few hours ahead of cooking time. Cream the butter until soft, then gradually beat in the mustard, lime juice, and cayenne pepper. Roll into a log shape and wrap in waxed paper. Refrigerate until needed.

2 Remove the skin from the chicken. Mix the wholegrain mustard, breadcrumbs, salt, and pepper. Melt the butter in a saucepan and add the breadcrumb mixture. Stir until all the breadcrumbs are coated with butter. Remove from the heat and leave to cool.

3 Preheat the oven to 400°F/200°C/Gas Mark 6. Put the flour into a bowl. Beat the eggs in another bowl. Take each drumstick and coat first with flour, then dip into the beaten egg, and finely press the breadcrumbs over the chicken.

4 Put the drumsticks on a greased baking tray and bake for 45 minutes. Alternatively, cook on a barbecue. Cut the lime and mustard butter into slices and serve with the chicken.

Serves 4

Tea-Smoked Chicken, Chinese Style

Ingredients
- 1 cooked (boiled) chicken (using fresh ginger in the cooking liquid)
- $1/2$ cup black tea leaves
- 2 tbsp brown sugar
- 1 tbsp oriental sesame oil

Method

1 Wipe the chicken well with paper towels and set it aside. Line the inside of a wok with several thicknesses of foil and add the tea leaves and brown sugar, mixing them together. Arrange a metal cake rack over the tea leaves and sugar so that they are close (about 2 in/5 cm away) but not touching.

2 Arrange the chicken on the rack, cover with a close-fitting lid or several thicknesses of foil, and heat over a moderate heat for 5 minutes. Once the tea mixture begins to smoke, keep over the heat, tightly covered, for a further 10 minutes.

3 Remove from the heat, turn the chicken carefully, cover tightly again, and smoke for a further 10–15 minutes. Remove from the heat and, without removing the cover, allow the chicken to stand for 15 minutes.

4 Remove the chicken and brush the skin all over with the sesame oil. Place on a cutting board and chop into small serving pieces before arranging on a serving plate.

Serves 6 part of a main meal

Stir-Fried Chicken Teriyaki

Ingredients

4 tbsp oil

4 tbsp light soy sauce

2 tbsp honey

1 tbsp mirin (rice wone) or dry sherry

2 cloves garlic, chopped

1 piece of fresh root ginger, grated

1 tsp dry mustard

4 chicken fillets, cut into strips

4 oz/125 g snow peas

½ cup sliced bamboo shoots

3 scallions, sliced

Method

1 Place the oil, soy sauce, honey, mirin or sherry, garlic, ginger and dry mustard in a large bowl; mix well. Stir the chicken into this marinade and coat well. Cover and chill for 1–2 hours.

2 Drain the chicken from the marinade and pour half the marinade into a heated wok. Add the drained chicken and stir-fry for 3–4 minutes or until the chicken changes color. Add the snow peas, bamboo shoots, and scallions and continue to stir-fry for a further 1–2 minutes or until the chicken is tender. Serve with a rice accompaniment.

Serves 4

Oven-Fried Lemon Chicken

Ingredients

2 x 2½ lb/1¼ kg chickens
1 cup flour
2 tsp salt
½ tsp pepper
1 tbsp paprika
2 x 2½ lb/1¼ kg chickens
6 oz/170 g butter or margarine

Sauce

1 tbsp soy sauce
1 tsp pepper
¼ cup oil
¼ cup lemon juice
1 tbsp grated lemon rind
2 cloves garlic, crushed

Method

1 Preheat the oven to 400°F/200°C/Gas Mark 6. Combine the flour, salt, pepper, and paprika. Cut the chicken into serving-sized pieces and toss in the seasoned flour. Grease a large ovenproof dish. Arrange the chicken pieces, skin-side down, in single layer. Melt the butter, spoon over the chicken, and bake, uncovered for 30 minutes. Turn the chicken, spoon the lemon sauce over and cook for a further 30 minutes or until tender, basting occasionally.

Note: Oven-fried lemon chicken is a succulent dish, perfect for entertaining. It can be made well in advance and just put in the oven when needed, leaving you plenty of time to talk to guests. Combine all the sauce ingredients, mix well, and refrigerate for 1 hour.

Serves 4

These turkey recipes will show you how to make the most of the bird once you catch it. Spread your wings with Turkey Fajitas and Turkey Creole. Finish the season on a high with roast turkey and all the trimmings; Your guests will be raving and your local poulterer will be giving you loyalty drumsticks!

Turkey

Turkey Steaks with Mustard Sauce

Ingredients

1 tbsp olive oil

4 skinless boneless turkey breast steaks, about 4 oz/125 g each

Sauce

½ oz/15 g sunflower spread

½ oz/15 g all-purpose flour

1¼ cups half-fat milk

1–2 tbsp wholegrain mustard

black pepper

fresh herbs, such as basil, chives or cilantro, to garnish

Method

1 Heat the oil in a non-stick frying pan. Add the turkey steaks and cook for 15 minutes or until tender and lightly browned, turning once.

2 Meanwhile, melt the sunflower spread in a saucepan. Add the flour and gently cook for 1 minute, stirring. Remove from the heat and gradually add the milk, stirring until smooth.

3 Return to the heat and slowly bring to the boil, stirring continuously, until the sauce thickens. Simmer for 2 minutes, stirring occasionally. Stir in the mustard and black pepper.

4 Spoon the mustard sauce over the turkey steaks and serve garnished with fresh herbs.

Note: Pan-fried turkey steaks served with a simple mustard sauce; what could be easier? New potatoes and lightly steamed leeks go particularly well with this dish.

Serves 4

Stuffed Turkey Breast Roll

Ingredients

1 turkey breast, approx 2½ lb/1¼ kg
salt and pepper

Stuffing

1 medium onion, finely chopped
2 cups fresh breadcrumbs
5 oz/145 g shaved ham, chopped
2 tbsp finely chopped parsley
2 tbsp Red Wine and Garlic Marinade

Red Wine and Garlic Marinade

½ cup red wine
¼ cup brown sugar
2 cloves garlic, crushed
salt and pepper

Method

1 Combine the marinade ingredients and set aside. Make a cut into the thick part of the breast, slanting the knife at a 45 degree angle and cutting almost through. Open out and pound the area with the side of a meat mallet to thin out evenly, then rub with salt and pepper. Mix the stuffing ingredients together and place along the center of the length. Form into a roll and secure with skewers. Tie with kitchen string at 1 in/2½ cm intervals then remove the skewers.

2 Cook as follows: For a kettle and gas hooded barbecue, prepare the barbecue for indirect heat medium-high. Oil the grill bars and place the turkey roll over the drip tray. Cover with the lid or hood and cook for 20 minutes, brushing with the marinade every 15 minutes until cooked when tested. The juices should run clear when pierced with a skewer. The total cooking time is approximately 1 hour.

For an electric barbecue grill with hood -preheat to roast temperature. Place the turkey roll in a foil dish and stand on a rack placed on the grill bars. Cover with the hood and cook as above.

3 Stand the turkey roll for 10 minutes before carving. Serve with glazed sweet potato and jacket potatoes. Mix the pan juices with a little marinade and serve as gravy.

Serves 6

Turkey and Mushroom Creole

Ingredients

1 tbsp olive oil

1 onion, chopped

2 cloves garlic, chopped

1 red bell pepper, deseeded and chopped

2 sticks celery, chopped

14 oz/400 g can chopped tomatoes

1 tsp chili powder

large pinch of cayenne pepper

1 tsp paprika

¼ tsp dried thyme

1 lb/450 g quick-cook turkey steaks, cut into strips

4 oz/125 g button mushrooms, sliced

Method

1 Heat the oil in a large heavy-based saucepan, then add the onion, garlic, red pepper, and celery, and cook gently for 10 minutes or until softened.

2 Stir in the tomatoes, chili, cayenne, paprika, and thyme and heat through for 1–2 minutes to release the flavors. Stir in the turkey strips and mushrooms, then cover the pan, and cook gently for 30 minutes, stirring occasionally, until the turkey is cooked through and tender.

Note: This West Indian-inspired dish tastes great and it's really healthy too. Serve it with some rice to soak up the spicy tomato and mushroom sauce.

Serves 4

Turkey Fajitas

Ingredients
1 lb/455 g turkey stir-fry strips
1 oz/30 g pack fajita seasoning mix
2 tbsp olive oil
8 Mexican flour tortillas
5½ fl oz/140 mL carton sour cream,
4 oz/120 g tub guacamole and lime wedges to serve

Salsa
2 ripe beefsteak tomatoes, finely chopped
1 small red onion, finely chopped
1 fresh red chili, deseeded and finely chopped
2 tbsp chopped fresh cilantro leaves
juice of 1 lime
pinch of sugar
salt and black pepper

Method

1 Place the turkey in a non-metallic bowl, add the fajita seasoning, and mix well. Cover and leave to stand. Meanwhile, place all the salsa ingredients in a bowl and stir in 1 tablespoon of the olive oil.

2 Heat a ridged cast-iron grill pan over a medium to high heat. Dip a folded piece of paper towel in the remaining oil and wipe it over the pan. Alternatively, heat the remaining oil in a heavy-based frying pan. Cook half the turkey, turning frequently, for 6 minutes or until golden. Transfer to a serving bowl and keep warm while you cook the remaining turkey, adding more oil to the pan if necessary.

3 Meanwhile, heat the tortillas according to the packet instructions, then pile them onto a serving plate. Spoon the salsa, sour cream, and guacamole into separate bowls and serve with the turkey, lime wedges, and tortillas.

Serves 4

Turkey Steaks with Balsamic Onions and Sweet Potato Mash

Ingredients

8 pickling onions halved, with the root intact

3 tbsp balsamic vinegar

1 tbsp brown sugar

4 (about 1 1/4 lb/600 g) turkey thigh steaks

canola cooking spray

1 1/2 lb/750 g orange sweet potato, peeled and chopped

3 tbsp chopped fresh dill

1 1/2 tbsp reduced-fat sour cream

2 oz/55 g baby spinach leaves, washed

Method

1 Put the pickling onions, vinegar, brown sugar, and 3 tablespoons of water in a frying pan. Stir over a low heat until the sugar dissolves, then cook, stirring occasionally, for 20 minutes or until the onions are soft and caramelized.

2 Trim the turkey steaks of any fat or sinew. Spray a large non-stick frying pan with canola spray and heat until hot. Cook the steaks over a medium-high heat for 5 minutes or until tender, turning once.

3 Cook the sweet potato in a large saucepan of boiling water until soft, drain, and return to the pan. Add the dill and sour cream, and mash until very smooth and creamy.

4 Layer the sweet potato, spinach leaves, turkey steaks, and balsamic onions on each plate.

Serves 4

Baked Pasta with Turkey and Cranberry

Ingredients

cooking spray

7 oz/200 g farfalle (butterfly or bow tie pasta)

3½ oz/100 g baby spinach leaves, washed

7 oz/200 g light turkey breast, shaved

6 eggs, lightly beaten

¼ cup low- or reduced-fat milk

⅓ cup grated reduced fat Cheddar cheese

2 tbsp cranberry sauce

Method

1 Preheat the oven to 350°F/180°C/Gas Mark 4. Spray 6 large (1 cup capacity) muffin tins with canola spray and line the bases with baking paper.

2 Cook the farfalle in a large pot of rapidly boiling water until just tender; drain well.

3 Line the bases and sides of the muffin tins with the farfalle. Steam the spinach until it wilts, drain well, and squeeze out any excess moisture.

4 Fill the center of each muffin tin with turkey breast and spinach.

5 Whisk together the eggs, milk, and cheese and pour into the muffin tins. Top with a spoonful of cranberry sauce. Bake for 20 minutes or until set. Turn out and serve with a green salad.

Makes 6

Turkey Fillets with Proscuitto

Ingredients

4 turkey fillets, about 3½ oz/100 g each
salt and black pepper
1 tbsp olive oil
16 fresh basil leaves
3½ oz/70 g pack proscuitto
2 oz/55 g Parmesan, freshly grated
⅓ cup dry white wine or chicken bouillon

Method

1 Preheat the oven to 375°F/190°C/Gas Mark 5. Place the turkey fillets between sheets of plastic wrap and pound with a rolling pin to flatten slightly. Unwrap the fillets, cut them in half widthways, and season. Heat the oil in a large heavy-based frying pan, then fry the fillets for 2 minutes on each side, until they are seared.

2 Arrange the fillets in a single layer in a baking dish. Place 2 basil leaves on each fillet, then crumple the proscuitto and lay it over the top. Sprinkle over the Parmesan.

3 Add the wine or bouillon to a frying pan and bring to the boil, stirring, then spoon over the turkey. Cover with foil and bake for 15 minutes. Remove the foil and cook for a further 5 minutes or until the cheese is golden brown.

Note: If you like Italian food, you'll love this dish. Made with proscuitto, Parmesan and basil, it scores low on effort but high on flavor. Serve with some crusty bread.

Serves 4

Game meats such as duck, quail and venison are perfect base for exotic dishes with international flavors. Complement the delicate flavors of game with just the right ingredients to create heart-warming meals such as Peking Duck Risotto and Venison with Cranberry and Red Wine Sauce.

Game

Fragrant Duck with Pineapple

Ingredients

- 2 boneless **Barbary duck breasts**, about 6 oz/170 g each, skinned and cut into strips
- 1 tsp five-spice powder
- 2 tbsp soy sauce
- 2 tbsp rice wine or dry sherry
- 1 tsp sugar
- 1 tbsp groundnut oil
- 1 orange or red bell pepper, deseeded and cut into thin strips
- 2 in/5 cm piece of fresh root ginger, cut into matchsticks
- 2 scallions, white and green parts separated, thinly shredded
- 6 oz/170 g fresh pineapple, cut into bite-sized pieces, plus juice
- salt

Method

1 Place the duck, five-spice powder, soy sauce, rice wine or sherry, and sugar in a shallow non-metallic bowl. Cover and marinate for 20 minutes.

2 Heat the oil in a wok. Remove the duck from the marinade and reserve the marinade. Stir-fry the duck over a high heat for 2 minutes. Add the pepper, ginger and the white scallions, and stir-fry for a further 3–4 minutes, until the pepper starts to soften.

3 Add the pineapple pieces and juice, and the marinade. Stir-fry for 1–2 minutes. Season with salt if necessary. Serve straight away, sprinkled with the green scallions.

Note: Fresh pineapple cuts through the richness of tender duck breasts marinated in Chinese spices. Serve this dish with plain boiled noodles or some fragrant jasmine rice.

Serves 4

Duck with Braised Turnips

Ingredients
4 duck leg joints
1 lb/500 g white turnips, peeled and cut into 2 in/5 cm chunks
salt and black pepper
½ cup chicken bouillon
1 tsp superfine sugar
1 tbsp fresh orange juice

Method

1 Preheat the oven to 375°F/190°C/Gas Mark 5. Heat a non-stick frying pan, add the duck, skin-side down, then cook over a medium-high heat for 7–8 minutes, until browned. Pour off the fat that runs out and reserve. Place the duck, skin-side up, on a baking tray and cook for 30–40 minutes, until the skin is crisp and the meat cooked through.

2 Meanwhile, cook the turnips in boiling salted water for 5–6 minutes, until softened, then drain. Place 2 tablespoons of the reserved duck fat in a large frying pan, add the turnips, and fry for 5 minutes or until lightly browned. Add the bouillon and season.

3 Partly cover the pan and cook for 10 minutes or until the turnips are tender and almost all the liquid has evaporated. Uncover the pan, add the sugar and orange juice, then cook over a high heat for 3–4 minutes, stirring, until the turnips caramelize. Serve with the duck.

Serves 4

Duck Breasts with Orange Sauce

Ingredients

4 boneless duck breasts, about 5 oz/145 g each

juice of 2 large oranges, plus a few strips of rind to garnish

1 green chili, deseeded and finely chopped

⅓ cup dry vermouth or sherry

1 tbsp redcurrant jelly

salt and black pepper

Method

1 Preheat the oven to 425°F/220°C/Gas Mark 7. Score the skin of each duck breast in a diamond pattern. Heat a heavy-based frying pan until hot, then place the breasts, skin-side down, in the pan. Cook over a medium to high heat for 5 minutes or until the skin is browned and crispy.

2 Pour off the hot fat, turn the duck over and cook for a further 5 minutes. Place the duck, skin-side up, on the rack of a roasting tin and cook in the oven for 10 minutes. Rest in a warm place for 5 minutes.

3 Meanwhile, make the dressing. Place the orange juice, chili, vermouth or sherry, redcurrant jelly, and seasoning in the pan. Boil vigorously, stirring constantly, for 5 minutes or until reduced and glossy.

4 Slice the duck very thinly. Serve with the sauce poured over and garnished with orange rind.

Note: Quickly pan-frying the duck, then roasting it, is a technique that a lot of chefs use to make the meat really succulent. Serve on a bed of bitter salad leaves or arugula.

Serves 4

Quail Portuguese

Ingredients

6–8 quail

thinly peeled zest of 1 orange

salt and fleshly ground pepper

1 oz/30 g butter

½ cup wine or orange juice

Rice Portuguese

1 onion, peeled and chopped

3 oz/85 g butter

2 cups long-grain rice

3 cups chicken bouillon, heated

2 tomatoes, peeled, seeded, and diced

1 red bell pepper, deseeded and diced

Method

1 Preheat the oven to 475°F/240°C/Gas Mark 9. Wipe over the quail, put a piece of orange zest in each, and season with salt and pepper. Tie into a neat shape with string and place in ovenproof casserole with the butter and wine or orange juice. Cover and cook in the oven for 20 minutes.

2 Meanwhile, make the Rice Portuguese. Fry the onion gently in half the butter until a golden color. Add the rice and cook, stirring, over a medium heat until the rice is coated with the butter. Add the hot bouillon, tomatoes, and pepper. Bring to the boil, reduce the heat, then cover with a lid and cook for about 18 minutes. As soon as the rice is cooked, carefully fork in the remaining butter.

3 Put the Rice Portuguese in a serving dish, then untie the quail and set it on top of the rice. Swirl the juices in the casserole to mix well; spoon over the rice.

Serves 4

Duck Legs with Orange and Olives

Ingredients

1 tbsp olive oil
6 duck legs, trimmed of excess fat
1 tsp black peppercorns, crushed
8 shallots, finely chopped
3 cloves garlic, finely chopped
2 cups white wine
finely grated rind of 1 orange
 and juice of 2 oranges
3 fresh rosemary sprigs,
 plus extra to garnish
3 oz/85 g pitted green olives
salt

Method

1 Heat the oil in a large, heavy-based saucepan, add the duck legs and fry for 5–6 minutes on each side, until browned. Remove and keep warm. Drain off all but a tablespoon of fat from the pan.

2 Add the peppercorns to the pan and fry for a few seconds, then add the shallots and garlic. Fry for 4 minutes or until the shallots start to color. Add the wine, orange juice, and rind, and bring to the boil. Reduce the heat and return the duck legs to the pan with the rosemary. Cover and simmer over a very low heat for 1½ hours or until the duck legs are tender and cooked through.

3 Transfer the duck legs to a serving dish and keep warm. Discard the rosemary and skim off as much fat as possible from the sauce. Add the olives and bring the sauce to the boil. Continue to boil for 10 minutes or until the sauce has reduced by about a third, then season with salt. Serve the duck legs with the sauce poured over, garnished with rosemary.

Note: Duck and orange is a classic combination and adding some olives makes it even better. Use chicken legs instead of duck if you like, but reduce the cooking time to 1 hour.

Serves 6

Thai Green Duck Curry with Bamboo Shoots

Ingredients

2 tbsp vegetable oil

3 tbsp Thai green curry paste

4 boneless duck breasts, skinned and cut into 1 in/2½ cm chunks

14 fl oz/400 mL can coconut milk

8 oz/225 g can sliced bamboo shoots, drained

2 tbsp fish sauce

1 tsp soft dark brown sugar

salt

3 tbsp chopped fresh basil, plus extra leaves to garnish

4 tbsp chopped fresh cilantro

Method

1 Heat the oil in a large, heavy-based saucepan, then add the curry paste and fry, stirring frequently, for 3 minutes or until the aromas are released. Add the duck, turn to coat thoroughly, then fry for 4–5 minutes, stirring from time to time.

2 Stir in the coconut milk, bamboo shoots, fish sauce, sugar, and salt to taste. Bring to the boil, stirring often, then reduce the heat. Simmer, uncovered, for 30–35 minutes, until the duck is tender, stirring occasionally. Just before serving, stir in the chopped basil and cilantro, and garnish with basil leaves.

Note: There's plenty of lemon grass in Thai green curry paste and its distinctive aroma and flavor make all the difference to this fabulous dish. Serve with noodles.

Serves 4

Peking Duck Risotto

Ingredients

1 cooked Peking duck
1 tbsp olive oil
1 tbsp toasted sesame oil
8 scallions, finely chopped
14 oz/400 g arborio rice
7 fl oz/200 mL dry white wine
2¾ cups rich duck bouillon
4 baby bok choy, halved or quartered lengthways
7 oz/200 g sliced water chestnuts, drained
3 tbsp fresh cilantro, chopped
3 tbsp fresh parsley, chopped
scallions greens to garnish
salt and pepper, to taste

Method

1 If the Peking duck is whole, cut it into manageable portions, and strip all the flesh from the bones, reserving the skin. Slice and set aside until required.

2 In a saucepan, heat the olive and sesame oils, and add the scallions. Cook gently for 2 minutes until softened, then add the rice and stir to coat. Add the wine and allow the liquid to absorb while stirring. Begin adding the bouillon, half a cup at a time, stirring very well after each addition and always allowing each previous quantity of bouillon to be absorbed before adding the next amount. With the second addition of bouillon, add the bok choy. When half the bouillon has been used, add the Peking duck and stir to incorporate. Continue adding bouillon in the usual manner.

3 With the last addition of bouillon, add the drained water chestnuts. When all the liquid has been absorbed, remove the pan from the heat. Add all the remaining fresh herbs and mix well. Serve the risotto garnished with the crispy duck skin.

Serves 4

327

Duck with Olives and Sherry

Ingredients

½ cup sliced or chopped large Spanish green olives
5 lb/2¼ kg duck, as much fat removed as possible
salt and freshly ground pepper
1 tbsp olive oil
1 medium onion, finely chopped
2 carrots, finely chopped
3 cloves garlic, minced
¾ cup chicken bouillon
¼ cup dry sherry or white wine
¼ tsp dried thyme
1 tbsp minced parsley

Method

1 Put olives in a small bowl, cover with warm water and set aside.

2 Preheat the oven to 350°F/180°C/Gas Mark 4. Sprinkle the duck inside and out with salt and pepper. Truss the duck, place it in a roasting pan, and prick it all over with a fork. Roast for 1 hour.

3 Meanwhile, heat oil in a shallow flameproof casserole, and sauté the onion, carrots, and garlic over medium-high heat until the onion has wilted.

4 Cut the duck into serving pieces, removing the backbone and rib cage and discarding them. Transfer the pieces to the casserole. Pour off the fat in the roasting pan and deglaze the pan with chicken bouillon, scraping up any particles stuck to the bottom. Strain the liquid into the casserole.

5 Drain the olives and add to the casserole along with the sherry, thyme, parsley, and salt and pepper. Bring to the boil on top of the stove, then cover, and cook in the oven for a further 1 hour.

Serves 4

Venison with Cranberry and Red Wine Sauce

Ingredients

4 tenderloin venison steaks, about 6 oz/170 g each
2 tbsp groundnut oil
juice of 1/2 orange and 1/2 lemon
1/2 tsp ground allspice
salt and black pepper
watercress to garnish

Sauce
2 tbsp groundnut oil
2 shallots, finely chopped
1 stick celery, finely chopped
1 carrot, finely chopped
1 cup red wine
1 cup beef bouillon
a few juniper berries
5 tbsp cranberry sauce

Method

1 Put the steaks into a non-metallic dish. Combine the oil, orange and lemon juice, allspice, and seasoning and pour over the steaks. Cover and marinate in the refrigerator for 4 hours, turning twice.

2 To make the sauce, heat the oil in a saucepan, add the shallots, celery, and carrot and cook gently, stirring occasionally, for 5 minutes or until lightly browned. Add the wine, bouillon, and berries and bring to the boil, then simmer for 20 minutes or until reduced by about half. Strain into a clean pan, add the cranberry sauce, and set aside.

3 Preheat the broiler to medium. Place the steaks on a rack and grill for 4–6 minutes on each side, until cooked. Meanwhile, reheat the sauce, stirring occasionally, until the cranberry sauce has melted. Season to taste, then spoon the sauce over the steaks and garnish with watercress.

Note: Richly flavored venison is just the thing for an autumn or winter dinner party. Serve it on a bed of celeriac and potato mash, with some carrots or a green vegetable.

Serves 4

331

Venison Casserole with Chili Beans

Ingredients

2 tbsp all-purpose flour

salt and black pepper

2 x 11 oz/310 g packs diced shoulder of venison

2 tbsp groundnut oil

1 Spanish onion, finely chopped

2 cloves garlic, crushed

2 fresh green chilies, deseeded and finely chopped

1 tbsp chili powder

14 oz/400 g can chopped tomatoes

14 fl oz/400 mL beef bouillon

2 tbsp tomato paste

2 tsp soft light or dark brown sugar

14 oz/400 g can red kidney beans, drained and rinsed

Method

1 Preheat the oven to 150°C/300°F/Gas Mark 2. Mix together the flour, salt, and pepper on a plate. Dip the venison into the mixture to coat. Heat the oil in a large flameproof casserole dish and fry the venison in batches over a medium to high heat for 5 minutes, or until browned on all sides. Remove from the pan and set aside.

2 Lower the heat and add the onion to the dish with a little more oil, if necessary. Stir for 5 minutes or until lightly browned, then add the garlic, chilies, and chili powder, and stir for 1 minute.

3 Add the tomatoes, beef bouillon, tomato paste and sugar. Bring to the boil, stirring. Add the venison, stir well, and cover tightly with the lid. Transfer the dish to the oven and cook for 2 hours or until the venison is tender, stirring twice and adding the kidney beans for the last 30 minutes of cooking.

Serves 4

Index

Asian chicken and kaffir lime salad	188
Australian-style chicken curry	254
Baked conchiglie with sausages and mustard	164
Baked pasta with turkey and cranberry	308
Barbecued chicken and mushroom patties	213
Barbecued leg of lamb in paper	104
Beef appetizers, snacks, & salads	**12**
Beef carpaccio	16
Beef	**10**
Beef-filled cucumber boats with dipping sauce	20
Beef mains	**30**
Beef with green peppercorn sauce and potatoes	38
Beef with wine sauce	44
Boiled beef and vegetables	52
Corn and bacon flan	156
Chicken and endive salad with creamy dressing	182
Chicken and pear curry	278
Chicken and vegetable stir-fry	270
Chicken fingers	200
Chicken focaccia with marinated vegetables	204
Chicken, leek, and mushroom flan	224
Chicken maryland	246
Chicken parmigiana	222
Chicken puff pie	218
Chicken rissoles	206
Chicken rolls with an Indonesian flavor	256
Chicken satay with crunchy cabbage salad	186
Chicken steaks with herb sauce	248
Chicken storage and cooking guide	**8**
Chicken supreme	274
Chicken vegetable soup	184
Chicken wings Moroccan style	262
Chicken with mustard	288
Chicken with oregano and lemon	286
Chicken with ricotta, arugula, and roast bell pepper	284
Chili con carne	26
Chorizo and lentil stew	162
Coconut curry	232
Cilantro shanks	80
Creamy chicken pasta	266
Creamy mustard chicken	236
Creamy pepper steak	56
Crisp chicken	244
Crisp curried wings with steamed rice	194
Crunchy chicken and potato salad	190
Crunchy drumsticks	196
Curried chicken	264
Curried chicken salad	192
Drumsticks in tomato sauce	260
Duck breasts with orange sauce	318
Duck legs with orange and olives	322
Duck with braised turnips	316
Duck with olives and sherry	328
Easy apricot and mango chicken loaf	240
Easy chicken stir-fry	232
Easy crumbed chicken	178
Feta drumsticks	236
Fire and spice risotto	42
Fragrant duck with pineapple	314
Game	**312**
Ginger wings	210
Glazed corned beef	46

Golden glazed drumsticks	202
Ground beef pie	46
Ham and cheese tortellini with sage butter	146
Ham and mushroom filo tartlets	126
Hawaiian poached chicken	258
Hearty stew	58
Herb chutney chicken	244
Hokkien noodles with lemon grass chicken	268
Honey and sesame chicken	208
Honey-glazed thick straight sausages	170
Honeyed spare ribs	116
Hot chicken balls with salad and fruity sauce	206
Indian meatballs in tomato sauce	84
Individual beef and red wine pies	18
Irish stew	80
Italian sausage with zucchini and mezuma leaves	168
Keema curry	86
Lamb	**64**
Lamb mains	**78**
Lamb and lemon kebabs	**76**
Lamb and sweet potato stew	90
Lamb appetizers, soups, snacks, & salads	**66**
Lamb cutlets with olives	79
Lamb fillets with salsa pilaf	92
Lamb hotpot cooked in cider	96
Lamb racks with broad bean and pea purée	100
Lavash rolls	175
Lemon barbecue-roasted chicken with vegetables	216
Lemon grass beef parcels	22
Lemon grass pork skewers	112
Light chicken curry with jasmine rice	282
Lovely legs and vegetable casserole	238
Low-fat mini meatballs	76
Macaroni with lamb ragu	82
Meat-lovers, pizza	44
Meat storage & cooking guide	**6**
Mexican meat loaf	58
Middle-Eastern spinach and meatball soup	68
Mini beef and pine nut meat loaves	13
Moroccan harira	70
Moroccan lamb pizza	74
Moroccan stew	56
Mulligatawny	28
Nasi goreng	142
Orange-and-spice leg steaks	250
Oven-baked chicken schnitzels	230
Oven-fried lemon chicken	294
Pad Thai with pork and shrimp	140
Pasta bake	54
Pastitsio	36
Peking duck risotto	326
Peppered beef steaks with red onion salsa	50
Pesto-crusted racks of lamb	88
Poached chicken with tomato and mushroom sauce	252
Pork	**108**
Pork appetizers, snacks, & mains	**110**
Pork and mushroom kebabs with black olives	118
Pork and cilantro stir-fry	138
Pork and mushroom risotto	136
Pork appetizers, snacks & salads	110
Pork casserole	132
Pork fillet, noodle, and sugar snap stir-fry	158
Pork in walnut sauce	150
Pork loin steaks with fresh herbs and mustard	132

Pork mains	**130**
Pork mince and date burgers	120
Pork mini roast with lemon herbs	152
Pork pâté	122
Pork san choy bau	116
Pork steaks and salsa verde	134
Poultry	**172**
Poultry appetizers, snacks, & salads	**174**
Poultry mains	**212**
Poussins provençals	276
Quail Portuguese	320
Quick chicken lasagne	234
Quick sausage sizzle	166
Rich and tasty pork chops	131
Roast lamb with beans and tomatoes	94
Roasted honey pork scotch	148
Roasted leg of lamb with vegetables	102
Rosemary pork with lentils and apples	144
Sausages	**160**
Shepherd's pie	106
Sizzling beef	34
Slowly simmered Indonesian beef curry	48
South African bobotie	98
Southern barbecued chicken	214
Southern fried chicken drumsticks	198
Spaghetti bolognese	60
Spicy chicken burritos	220
Spicy lamb kebabs	67
Spicy satay skewers	176
Steak and kidney puffs	24
Steak au poivre	40
Stir-fried chicken teriyaki	292
Stir-fry chicken with almonds and broccoli	272
Stir-fry pork with water chestnuts	154
Stuffed turkey breast roll	300
Sweet and sour chicken	280
Tandoori chicken	228
Tandoori pork and mango pockets	114
Tangy tenderloins	242
Tea-smoked chicken, Chinese style	290
Thai beef salad	14
Thai chicken meatballs	180
Thai green duck curry with bamboo shoots	324
Thai pork sausage rolls	111
Turkey	**296**
Turkey and mushroom creole	302
Turkey fajitas	304
Turkey fillets with Parma ham	310
Turkey steaks with balsamic onions and sweet potato mash	306
Turkey steaks with mustard sauce	298
Turkish lamb boreklers	72
Veal saltimbocca	31
Veal schnitzel with glazed apricots	62
Veal with lemon, crisp sage, and cornmeal	32
Venison casserole with chili beans	332
Venison with cranberry and red wine sauce	330
Vineyard chicken	226
Warm lima bean and prosciutto salad with arugula	128
Warm vegetable salad with Serrano ham	124